Once for a Shining Hour

REFLECTIONS FOR CHRISTMAS

To George and Lib Watkins
Dear Lions friends –
We miss you

Once for a Shining Hour

REFLECTIONS FOR CHRISTMAS

Lawrence Webb
Lawrence Webb
Christmas 2013

CONNECTION PRESS
Anderson, South Carolina

Once for a Shining Hour: Reflections for Christmas
by Lawrence Webb
ISBN No. 978-1467988032

Book design by Nathan Golden
Cover art: istockphoto.com

Connection Press
Anderson, South Carolina

Bible passages are usually in italic to make them more readily identifiable.
Unless indicated otherwise, Bible passages are from the Revised Standard Version:
Revised Standard Version of the Bible, ©1952 [2nd edition, 1971]
by the Division of Christian Education of the National Council of the Churches of Christ
in the United States of America. Used by permission. All rights reserved.

"Christmas is Like Marriage" contains quotes by Rheta Grimsley Johnson's "Have
yourself a melancholy Christmas," an op-ed piece which appeared in The Anderson
Independent-Mail, Anderson, South Carolina, December 18, 1993.
These quotes are used with permission from Ms. Johnson.

"Not Your Usual Christmas Letter" contains quotes from R. Kirby Godsey's
When We Talk About God . . . Let's Be Honest. Macon, Georgia:
Smyth & Helwys Publishing Inc., 1996. These quotes are used with permission.

Additional copies may be ordered through:
www.amazon.com
www.createspace.com
McDowell's Emporium, 104 Oak Drive, Anderson, SC
Anderson County Museum, 202 East Greenville Street, Anderson, SC
Cards & Jewelry, 2925 North Main Street, Anderson, SC
B & R Books, 28 North Main Street, Honea Path, SC
Mountain Made, 102 Exchange Street, Pendleton, SC

Also by Lawrence Webb:
Christmas Memories: From Seven to Seventy
ISBN: 978-1-4392-1674-3

For Pansy
My companion and inspiration
through fortysome Christmas seasons

Table of Contents

Introduction

"It's the most *wonderful* time of the year," a song says about Christmas, and I agree. That's why I wrote this book. If you turn the word *wonderful* in that sentence around, you're saying, Christmas is "full of wonder." There's cause for eye-popping wonder when you consider the message of the New Testament Gospels: Jesus is "Emmanuel, God with us" (Matthew 1:23). He is the Eternal Word at one with God the Father, the Word who "became flesh and dwelt among us" (John 1:14). St. Paul is caught up in wonder as he considers the difference Jesus has made in his own life as he says, "Christ Jesus came into the world to save sinners." Then he adds, "of whom I am chief" (King James Version). Several modern-speech versions say, "and I am the worst" (1 Timothy 1:15).

Paul isn't bragging about setting the record as the world's worst sinner in his former life. He's ecstatic about how his life was turned around as he had a vision of Christ. This vision came, even as he was on his way to have Christian believers arrested or even killed *because* they believed.

In Luke's telling of the Christmas story, there is wondering and pondering (Luke 2:17-19). After the shepherds visit the manger and see the wonderful Child, we are told, *they made known the saying which had been told them concerning this child; and all who heard it wondered at what the shepherds told them.* Some translations describe this wonder as amazement and astonishment. We also see Mary's response: *Mary kept all these things, pondering them in her heart.*

So, yes, Christmas *is* "the most wonderful time of the year" to me because of the birth of Jesus and the difference He makes in my life and can make in yours.

The songwriter sees a wonderful time in jingle bells, holiday greetings, happy meetings, parties, marshmallows, caroling, mistletoe, hearts a glow, and loved ones near at hand. Lots of activities which gladden our spirits and stir up warm fuzzies. You and I can find wonder in some or all of those things. But as you read the lyrics carefully, you realize there's only one angling reference to Christmas and no mention of Jesus at all.

Come to think of it, that's a pretty accurate description of Christmas in America. It's easy to have a wonderful time with the holidays and never get around to Jesus. That's another reason I wrote this book. These reflections acknowledge the tension or undercurrent we feel as we try to balance the social holiday wonder with the wonder at the Word who became flesh.

The essays draw their inspiration from varied sources:
* Songs of the season, old and new, sacred and secular, from Canada, Britain, and the U. S.
* Texts of two new Christmas hymns I have written, set to familiar tunes

* A Christmas quote from *Hamlet* in a secular television drama
* The true story of soldiers who stopped fighting to celebrate Christmas Eve and Christmas Day
* John Grisham's seriocomic novel about a man who tries to skip Christmas
* Grumblings of a grade school boy who is forced to take a bath
* Rheta Grimsley Johnson's newspaper column comparing Christmas with marriage
* A Holiday visit to a bombed-out British cathedral
* A painting in a London church basement
* My little granddaughter's first part in a pageant
* A family Christmas letter telling about the young husband's bout with cancer
* Classic Christmas stories: Charles Dickens's *A Christmas Carol*, Henry Van Dyke's "The Story of the Other Wise Man," and O. Henry's "The Gift of the Magi"
* A play about men who remember Christmas while they are prisoners of terrorists
* Plus a few of my personal memories spanning childhood, youth, and adult years
* The title essay in the collection is taken from the plainest of tree decorations--a clear plastic disc with these words: "Once for a shining hour, heaven touched the earth." That statement grabs my heart and shakes tears of joy from it.

I pray these essays will provide food for your thoughts – perhaps some you will need to chew on a while – and that they will help make your Christmas "the most wonderful time of the year."

He Who Built the Starry Skies

Lo, within a manger lies He who built the starry skies...[1]

THESE WORDS WERE WRITTEN by 19th century British songwriter Edward Caswall. The builder in question is Jesus. We don't usually associate the Babe in the manger of Bethlehem with hammer and nails. On the other hand, we know when Jesus grows up, He is identified as a carpenter (Mark 6:3).

These startling words about the Celestial Carpenter are from Caswall's carol, "See Amid the Winter's Snow," with the alternate title, "Hymn for Christmas Day."

I first became aware of this song on a CD titled, *Christmas from English Cathedrals.* The CD, produced in 1998, features ten carols from four different cathedrals. The St. Paul Cathedral Choir in London sings "See Amid the Winter's Snow."

The depiction of the birth of Jesus as happening in snowy weather strains credulity when you realize the little town of Bethlehem is approximately on the same latitude as Waycross in deep south Georgia, where snow is rare. So our impressions of white Christmases come more from Jolly Old England or New England rather than from Holy Writ. But that's not all bad. If we see the coming of Jesus in terms of our own environment and our own times, that coming can be much more personal. If we can picture His entrance into our own time and our own weather conditions, this transforms the story. In that way, what we may have viewed as a pleasant tale from the ancient past has resonance and relevance for our own time.

Ken Gire seems to echo Caswall's thought in a meditation on Mary and Joseph in his book, *Intimate Moments with the Savior.* Writing of Mary and her newborn Son, Gire says, "She touches his tiny hand. And hands that once sculpted the mountain ranges cling to her finger."[2]

These pictures from Edward Caswall's song and Ken Gire's meditation throw us off stride. We say we believe Jesus is God's revelation in human form. But it's hard to come to terms with these vivid assertions in song and prose, even though they are saying what we claim to believe about Jesus.

If we review the Four Gospels in the order in which they probably were written, the writers of the Gospels, each in turn, seem to give more information about Jesus as "He who built the starry skies" or the tiny hands in the manger as the "hands that once sculpted the mountain ranges."

Mark is widely regarded as the first Gospel because it is obvious that Matthew and Luke use Mark as their outline and then add material of their own. John is generally considered the latest of the four. If we follow this timeframe, we can see a progression of assertions regarding the nature of Jesus and His relation to all humanity and to the Creator God:

Mark, as the earliest, gives no birth details. Rather, he

plunges directly into the ministry of Jesus in 1:1, *The beginning of the gospel of Jesus Christ, the Son of God.* This is followed immediately with the introduction of John the Baptist and Jesus's own baptism. The words in that opening sentence are exciting and provocative as they refer to Jesus as the Christ and the Son of God. To say Jesus is "Christ" is to say He is the long-hoped-for Messiah because "Christ" is simply the Greek equivalent for the Hebrew word "Messiah," the promised deliverer.

Calling Jesus "the Son of God" is not identical with saying He is God. But this term indicates Jesus is from God and that He stands in a special relationship with God as His Father.

Matthew, for several reasons, is generally regarded as written for a Jewish audience. One example is the thirteen times this Gospel points to events in the birth, ministry, and death of Jesus as fulfillment of Hebrew Scripture.

The first stanza of Caswall's carol picks up on this as it points to Jesus as the fulfillment of prophecy:

See the tender Lamb appears, Promised from eternal years.

The prophecies Matthew uses include the virgin birth as fulfillment of Isaiah 7:14. While some newer versions translate this passage differently and minimize the idea of this literal prediction, the traditional King James Version shows how Matthew uses this passage: *Behold, a virgin shall conceive and bear a son, and shall call his name Immanuel, a name which means "God with us."* Matthew cites this passage, stating in 1:22, *All this took place to fulfil what the Lord had spoken by the prophet.*

So Matthew wants his readers to see Jesus in a Jewish

context. To set that mood, the opening words of this Gospel link Jesus with King David and with Abraham, the father of the Jewish faith: *The book of the genealogy of Jesus Christ, the son of David, the son of Abraham* (1:1).

The ancestral listing begins with Father Abraham and moves down the generations, climaxing with these words: . . . *and Jacob the father of Joseph the husband of Mary, of whom Jesus was born, who is called the Christ* (1:16). Thus, Matthew traces Jesus back to Abraham, the man who stands at the head of the Jewish people.

Luke makes a broader appeal. This author is generally considered to have been a a non-Jew, a Gentile. Like Matthew, Luke tells of the virgin-born Savior, in this case, announced by angels to the shepherds in the field. Luke also gives a genealogy in chapter 3, but he reverses Matthew's chronological pattern, starting with Jesus and working back: *Jesus, when he began his ministry, was about thirty years of age, being the son (as was supposed) of Joseph, the son of Heli . . .* (3:23). But, rather than stopping with the Jewish patriarch, Abraham, Luke takes the list as far as we can go, humanly speaking, and then goes even further, back to *the son of Enos, the son of Seth, the son of Adam, the son of God* (3:38).

John is almost universally acknowledged among scholars as the latest and is often referred to simply as "the Fourth Gospel." In this Fourth Gospel, the writer starts where Luke stops, namely with God the Creator and the beginning of all things:

In the beginning was the Word, and the Word was with God, and the Word was God. He was in the beginning with God; all things were made through him, and without him was not anything made that was made (1:1-2).

In verse 14. John clearly identifies this Word who was from the very beginning:

And the Word became flesh and dwelt among us, full of grace and truth; we have beheld his glory, glory as of the only Son from the Father.

So there is no question that John is describing one who is Very God of Very God come to earth as a human being. That One is Jesus whom the earlier Gospels have portrayed both as Son of God in Mark and as the son of an earthly virgin mother in Matthew and Luke.

We recognize, then, that the lines from Edward Caswall's song and Ken Gire's prose spring full-grown from the first and third verses of John:

In verse 1 of John, the Eternal Word was in the beginning with God, and, indeed, the Word *was* God. Then, verse 3 declares this Eternal Word (Jesus) to have been a partner in creating all things. This, then is a biblical foundation for those Christmas lyrics:

Lo, within a manger lies He who built the starry skies...

A less well-known passage in Colossians 1:15-20 is even more elaborate in its assertion that Jesus is at one with God and that He was active in creating everything:

He is the image of the invisible God, the first-born of all creation; for in him all things were created, in heaven and on earth, visible and invisible, whether thrones or dominions or principalities or authorities -- all things were created through him and for him. He is before all things, and in him all things hold together. He is the head of the body, the church; he is the beginning, the first-born from the dead, that in everything he might be pre-eminent. For in him all the fulness of God was pleased to dwell, and through him to reconcile to himself all things, whether on earth or in heaven, making peace by the blood of his cross.

That theme is restated later in Colossians 2:9-10: *For in him the whole fulness of deity dwells bodily, and you have come to fulness of life in him, who is the head of all rule and authority.*

Despite these ringing affirmations from Christian Scripture, those who are inclined to walk more by sight rather than by faith find Jesus the Eternal Architect impossible to believe.

Within contemporary biblical scholarship, there is a branch of scholars who reject the miraculous element. Passages emphasizing the virgin birth and Jesus as eternally pre-existent are rejected out of hand. If biblical stories or sermons cannot be explained by modern reason, they are declared invalid.

In Lewis Carroll's *Through the Looking Glass,* the White Queen tells Alice things which Alice says she can't believe. The Queen says when she was Alice's age, she used to spend half an hour a day believing impossible things, and "sometimes I've believed as many as six impossible things before breakfast." [3]

We need not relegate matters of faith to the junk pile. Life is full of marvels which the human mind will never fully comprehend. We need not equate the unseen or inexplicable with the realm of believing "six impossible things before breakfast."

In "See Amid the Winter's Snow," after the introductory assertion that "he who built the starry skies" is lying in a manger, the one who has been "promised from eternal years," the song becomes a question and answer time between the shepherds of

Bethlehem and an unidentified interrogator.

Say, ye holy shepherds, say/What your joyful news today; Wherefore have ye left your sheep/ On the lonely mountain steep?

The shepherds explain:

"As we watched at dead of night, Lo, we saw a wondrous light; Angels singing peace on earth Told us of the Saviour's birth"

The recurring chorus greets the blessed day of His birth as the dawn of redemption:

Hail, thou ever-blessed morn! Hail, redemption's happy dawn! Sing through all Jerusalem, Christ is born in Bethlehem.

Skeptics cannot disprove what is said to have happened that night on Bethlehem's hillside and in the manger near the inn. Neither can the faithful prove these stories scientifically. But the ear of faith can hear "Glory to God in the highest" echoing from the Judean hills, and the eye of faith can look with awe at the stable bed and declare

Lo, within a manger lies He who built the starry skies...

---

[1] All the lyrics quoted from Edward Caswall's "See Amid the Winter's Snow" are found at
http://www.cyberhymnal.org/htm/s/e/seeamid.htm.

[2] Ken Gire, *Intimate Moments with the Savior*. Grand Rapids, Mich.: Zondervan Publishing House, 1989, p. 5.

[3] http://www.sabian.org/looking_glass5.php.

Christmas is Like Marriage

"CHRISTMAS IS A LOT LIKE A MARRIAGE. For a good one you have to work at it. You have to really want it. And I don't want to divorce Christmas, despite the grim headlines and sad stories and gross commercialization. I don't even want a trial separation. I want to work things out, to see it through, to rekindle the lost spark."

So said syndicated columnist Rheta Grimsley Johnson [1] as she thought of all the bad news in the lead-up to December 25: traffic accidents, random murders on a commuter train, word of a friend's longtime marriage ending in divorce. Such things happen all through the year, but the tragedies seem magnified when they occur as Christmas approaches.

Ms. Johnson also felt pulled in two directions in terms of making Christmas work: on the one hand, buying expensive gifts for friends and associates and pampering herself as well; on the other hand, giving of herself through home-crafted gifts and working in a soup kitchen on Christmas Day.

Anyone who's been married even a few weeks probably

realizes it takes work to make a go of it. But some who have lived through decades and decades of Christmas seasons may never have thought of applying that same principle to Christmas observance.

If we accept Ms. Johnson's premise that Christmas really is a lot like a marriage and that one has to work at either one, we need to determine what it takes to succeed. The columnist suggested the essence of success in her mention of things she knew she ought to do, namely, giving of herself to other people.

We can elaborate on that a bit by noting the basic work which makes for a lasting marriage: mutual love and respect that manifests itself through practical details making life happier and easier for the marriage partner. Those same principles can also be applied to make Christmas "work" for us.

Jack Carmine and Linda Lobo, characters in Robert James Waller's novel *Border Music*, are amazed when they meet the Thorvalds, a couple celebrating their fortieth anniversary. Jack and Linda have no permanence in their personal relationship or in places where they live together. With exaggeration, Jack says if he were to add up the married years of everyone he knows, including those who've been married two or three times, the total wouldn't even be forty. As they look at the Thorvalds who are smiling at each other, Jack and Linda see in their faces that they've spent years working it out and making it work.[2] In keeping with Rheta Johnson's metaphor, perhaps Jack and Linda resemble people who don't quite know how to deal with marriage or Christmas.

In her column, Ms. Johnson noted things she could do as part of the work which is required: make a few presents, write letters and make short visits to make Christmas a good one for other people.

From her comment that she didn't want to divorce herself from Christmas, we infer that the tension she mentioned is real in her life, that she recognizes it takes hard work to keep the "gross commercialization" from winning the day. As the shopping season kicks into high gear and we are bombarded by ads on the Internet, TV, and radio, we also are surrounded by friends, family, and colleagues whose attitudes and actions express competing definitions. To take lines from poet Rudyard Kipling out of context, "If you can keep your head when all about you/ Are losing theirs . . ."[3] amid the maelstrom of the buildup to Christmas, you probably will not sue for divorce.

Perhaps you are reading this in the early days of Advent. If so, let me suggest some things you could do from now to Christmas to make Christmas work for you and for those you love – and even for some you hardly know who would like for Christmas to be more workable for them. Some of these you could do every day. Others would probably be done once during the season. You probably would not attempt to do everything on this list:

1. Read, sing, or play a recording of Christmas carols. With your family, or if you live alone, you might play a CD or cassette of sacred Christmas music at mealtimes.

2. Write a letter or send a card to a person who made an earlier Christmas special for you. I recently traveled to see my college freshman English professor after many years and told him how much his encouragement has meant to me across the decades.

3. Call or visit someone who is homebound and

express appreciation for friendship or concern for that person's well being.

4. Sit quietly and think of times when God has been real and near in your life.

5. Write down your thoughts which came to mind as you took the previous action.

6. Surprise your spouse or your children or a good friend by cooking his (her or their) favorite meal.

7. Try to develop the skill and patience to listen carefully to those closest to you to try to discover their needs and longings.

8. Visit someone who lives alone. If that person offers to do something for you, let her. Fred Craddock tells of having Sunday dinner with a widow in a church where he was the guest preacher. As she prepared an elaborate meal and put out her best silver and china, he insisted she should not go to such trouble. After he had his say, the woman told him it had been years since she had been able to prepare and share a meal with anyone, so he should sit back and hush while she finished her preparation.

9. Go caroling with a group from your church or club or neighborhood. Select people to sing to those who live alone or who have difficulty getting away from the house.

10. With friends, plan a "Mother's Morning (or Afternoon) Out," to give mothers with small children opportunity to get away for a few hours.

11. Address and deliver Christmas cards to residents in a retirement home or a home for veterans.

12. Bake a plate of cookies or brownies for members of an older Sunday school class at your church. If you don't bake, go

to the bakery department of your super market.

13. Invite a lonely person in for a cup of coffee or tea. Or take that person to a restaurant or coffee shop.

14. Find TV listings for programs which present the Christian meaning of Christmas and watch some of these.

15. Read Charles Dickens's *A Christmas Carol* (the story of Ebenezer Scrooge).

16. Watch a video of *A Christmas Carol* or the Jimmy Stewart movie, *It's a Wonderful Life.*

17. Try your hand with writing a Christmas poem to share with your family or to put on your original Christmas cards.

18. Read Christmas stories to neighborhood children.

19. Attend a music program or pageant at your church or a neighboring church.

20. If you have any musical talent but haven't been singing in a choir, ask a church choir director to let you join them for the Christmas music.

21. Through your church or civic club, prepare a meal for homeless people.

22. Invite a person who lives alone to Christmas dinner.

23. Volunteer at a homeless shelter.

24. Pray daily for those you are trying to befriend through these helpful actions.

25. Read a Bible passage every day from now through Christmas, such as those listed at the end of this essay. They include Hebrew Scriptures which look with hope to the coming Messiah and New Testament passages with details of the coming of Jesus.

If you follow the suggestions listed here for a good Christmas – even a few of them – it will take work. But, as

Ms. Johnson pointed out, "For a good one you have to work at it. You have to really want it." With actions such as these, we will "...work things out, to see it through, to rekindle the lost spark."

Two Bible passages come to mind that point to helpful work in the name of God which apply to Christmas and any time of the year:

> *Every one helps his neighbor, and says to his brother, "Take courage!"* (Isaiah 41:6).

> *"And Peter opened his mouth and said: . . . 'God anointed Jesus of Nazareth with the Holy Spirit and with power; how he went about doing good and healing all that were oppressed by the devil, for God was with him'"* (Acts 10:34, 38).

If our Christmas activity includes helping our neighbors, and if we follow the example of Jesus, *how he went about doing good*, we will make it work and will not want to divorce Christmas.

Suggested daily Bible readings:

(1) Isaiah 9:1-7	(14) Luke 1:26-33
(2) Isaiah 40:1-5	(15) Luke 1:34-38
(3) Isaiah 40:9-11	(16) Luke 1:39-45
(4) Isaiah 60:1-3	(17) Luke 2:1-7
(5) Micah 5:1-5	(18) Luke 2:8-14
(6) Malachi 3:1-4	(19) Luke 2:15-20
(7) Malachi 4:1-6	(20) John 1:1-5
(8) Matthew 1:18-25	(21) John 1:10-14

(9) Matthew 2:1-6   (22) John 3:16-18
(10) Matthew 2:7-12   (23) Philippians 2:5-11
(11) Matthew 2:13-15   (24) Colossians 2:6-10
(12) Matthew 2:16-18   (25) Hebrews 1:1-4
(13) Matthew 2:19-23

---

[1] Rheta Grimsley Johnson, "Have yourself a melancholy Christmas," *The Anderson Independent-Mail*, Anderson, South Carolina, Opinion Page, December 18, 1993. Quoted by permission from Ms. Johnson.

[2] Robert James Waller, *Border Music*, published 1995. www.fictiondb.com/author/robert-james-waller~24246.htm

[3] "If," by Rudyard Kipling www.poemhunter.com/poem/**if**

Glory to God in the Highest

In a children's Christmas program at church, Little Addie, a very active three and a half years old, was the youngest of the angels. She had one line from Scripture: "Glory to God in the highest." So when her time came, she went to the microphone to have her say.

The mic was a tad tall for a girl who was three and a half. So she tugged at it in the effort to get it to her level. After doing the best she could, Addie said, "Glory to God in the highest." That should have been the end of Addie's solo performance, but she wasn't satisfied with the way it had gone. So she said, as before, "Glory to God in the highest."

That still didn't come out to her satisfaction, so once again, she planned to say those words from the angels: "Glory to God in the highest." By now, some of the other kids were getting tired of Addie's hogging the microphone. Finally, an older girl stepped over to try to get Addie away from the mic so the rest of the cast could have their turns. After a bit of a tussle, this Littlest Angel was led away, and the show went on.

That little performance got widespread exposure. I saw it on *YouTube* along with hundreds of other amused viewers.

Obviously, Addie didn't understand the entire plan for Christmas program. She knew her one part of the angel's greeting. Other parts went by, unnoticed.

I tell you this story for two reasons: For one thing, Addie is my granddaughter.

Also, the message from that Littlest Angel is the climax of the message from a sky full of angels with the promise of joy for all people from Luke 2. The larger passage is directed to shepherds who are keeping their vigil on a cold, dark night. That message begins with reassurance and a promise:

Be not afraid; for behold, I bring you good news of a great joy which will come to all the people.

The men have good reason to be afraid because, Luke tells us, *an angel of the Lord appeared to them, and the glory of the Lord shone around them, and they were filled with fear.*

In the old faithful King James Bible, when the shepherds saw the angel, *they were sore afraid.* The comedian Brother Dave Gardner from the 1960s said, if you're "sore afraid," that means you're scared to death. But with the shepherds, it's probably more than that. George Bliss suggests this is "the awe which smites the mind" when we are struck with a sense of the "nearness of God."[1]

But the angel tries to calm the shepherds, assuring them that he has come with a message they need to hear: *I bring you good news of a great joy which will come to all the people.* So this is a message for everyone, not just for those smelly sheep herders working the night shift in the rough countryside on the outskirts of Bethlehem.

Our daughter-in-law, Nurse Vicky, Addie's mother, has the night shift at an obstetric hospital, more or less permanently, and seems to manage pretty well. But nighttime can be pretty scary if you're out in the dark. You're looking and listening, half expecting something to happen or someone to come around to bother you.

Sure 'nuff, as these rugged men sit out there in the night, trying to outdo one another with their tall tales of spooks and apparitions, someone *does* come around to unsettle them. And it's not an ordinary someone. It's an angel of the Lord. Luke says *the glory of the Lord shone around them.*

The angels' appearance to the shepherds was in itself a fulfillment of the promise that this good news was to be for all people.

The promise that this good news is for all people means salvation is for the Down and Out and the Up and Out alike. Whatever our financial or educational standing, we are all on level ground before God. And that is part of the message of great joy to all people.

That great joy also extends to all races and national backgrounds, all colors, all languages, all religions and no religions, all political persuasions. All of that is at the core of great joy for all people. If language means anything, ALL people means ALL people. Not *some* people. Not just folks we consider OUR kind of people, but ALL people, starting with those dirty shepherds who got the first word that a Savior is born in the little town of Bethlehem. The Christmas story also includes those men of wealth who traveled a long distance, carrying gifts of gold, frankincense and myrrh. *[G]ood news... to all the people...*

For to you is born this day in the city of David a Savior, who is Christ the Lord.

The city of David is Bethlehem.

To say this baby is the Savior for all people means He will be the universal Deliverer from sin.

Stop to remember, the word *Christ* is simply the Greek equivalent of the Hebrew word *Messiah*. the Promised One, the Long-Hoped-For One. Then, to call Jesus Lord is to declare Him to be at one with God.

So that is a threefold description of this Newborn Babe: Savior, Christ, and Lord.

That triple description may seem off-putting for these simple men of the land. But when the angel tells the shepherds how they can track down and identify this Wonder Child, they can certainly identify with Him:

And this will be a sign for you: you will find a babe wrapped in swaddling cloths and lying in a manger."

Not in the most comfortable room in the best inn Bethlehem can provide. But around on the backside of nowhere, lying in a trough the animals feed from. That's the realm these shepherds are familiar with.

So the shepherds will rush off in a moment to look for this Savior who is Christ the Lord. But not before we get back to Little Addie's exclamation: *Glory to God in the highest*. Addie's words did not come from one lone three-and-a-half year old, or from one lone angel, for that matter:

And suddenly there was with the angel a multitude of the heavenly host praising God and saying, "Glory to God in the highest, and on earth peace among men with whom he is pleased!"

As we seek that joy which the angels proclaimed to those

ancient shepherds – joy that will be to all people – we need to distinguish joy from happiness. Julie Yarborough, a minister in New Jersey, drew a distinction between joy and happiness:

We're happy when things go our way, but joy comes from knowing "the presence of God-with-us at all times." We can celebrate joy, "even in the midst of grief and sadness." She also said joy "can erupt in a depressed economy, in the middle of a war, in an intensive care waiting room." [2]

United Methodist pastor Dean Snyder in the Georgetown section of our nation's capital, continued the contrast between happiness and joy:

Joy is not something we can buy or sell or steal. It's not discounted at your favorite department store. It can't be downloaded or legislated or won in a lawsuit. It can't be earned or inherited or turned on with a remote control. [3]

Noted preacher and writer Frederick Buechner gives further contrast between joy and happiness:

Happiness comes from things we do, things we have: a satisfying job, a loving relationship, money, a vacation, or good health. But joy is unpredictable. We can try to achieve happiness, but joy is something we can only receive. [3]

Perhaps we can contrast happiness and joy as we think further about the shepherds of Bethlehem. These men are happy as they run to the manger. Luke records that trip, beginning in verse 15:

When the angels went away from them into heaven, the shepherds said to one another, "Let us go over to Bethlehem and see this thing that has happened, which the Lord has made known to us." And they went with haste, and found Mary and Joseph, and the babe lying in a manger. And when they saw it they made known the saying which had been told them concerning this child; and all who heard it wondered at what the shepherds told them.

The shepherds realize something deep and significant is unfolding before them as they run into town. No doubt, this makes them happy to be on the scene of something that defies explanation.

Then, after a while, when the excitement dies down and they are back in the routine of tending sheep, something of a deeper level of awareness sets in. Then they begin to reflect on all they have heard from the angels and have seen for themselves with Mary and Joseph and the Holy Child. At that point, I believe we can say the shepherds move from happiness to joy.

When they begin to realize the difference this will make in their lives, that's when joy sets in. The initial happiness will die out when the excitement cools down after that night with the angels and the Babe in the Manger. But as they consider the difference this good news can make, their long nights on the hillside will have new significance.

Luke's last word about the shepherds in verse 20 gives us a clue to their new-found joy:

And the shepherds returned, glorifying and praising God for all they had heard and seen, as it had been told them.

The shepherds echo the words of the angels, and perhaps we can hear echoes of a three-and-a-half year old as she, too, glorifies God as best she knows how, with her "Glory to God in the highest!"

My little granddaughter didn't see the larger picture. If you had quizzed her about her speech, she likely would've had difficulty explaining why the angels were singing, "Glory to God in the highest!" But she took the part and said her one line – more than once – at her own level of understanding. And that's what we all do: think on our own level about Jesus coming into the world.

---

[1] George R. Bliss, "Luke," *An American Commentary on the New Testament*, Volume II. Philadelphia: American Baptist Publication Society, 1884, p. 46.

[2] Julie Yarborough, "True Joy," December 13, 1998, Summit, New Jersey. christchurchsummit.org

[3] Dean Snyder, "Making Way for Joy," Foundry United Methodist Church, Georgetown, Washington, D.C., December 8, 2002. http://www.foundryumc.org/sermons/12 8 2002. pdf.

Christmas at Coventry

PANSY AND I HAVE SEEN ANCIENT RUINS in many places around England, often amid contrasting modern structures. One of our more memorable visits to a church in ruins was at Coventry, which is the site of a post-World War Two contemporary-design cathedral alongside the remains of a building which dates back to medieval times.

Coventry's historic cathedral didn't simply fall into disrepair across the centuries. It fell in one night – November 14, 1940 – as bombs from Hitler's air force destroyed much of the city.

In the aftermath of a war's destruction, survivors in many cultures vow never to forget or forgive. Hate-filled memories are kept alive for decades, even centuries. The Civil War is still being fought in some sections of the United States after a century and a half. In the British Isles, hostilities endure across many centuries between the Scots and the English, the Irish and English, and even within the borders of Northern Ireland between Protestants and Catholics.

When we visited Coventry during a Christmas season,

we learned of a more hopeful story which emerged from the devastation there. We rode a bus from Stratford-Upon-Avon, Shakespeare's hometown, where we were staying in a bed and breakfast. It was only a nineteen-mile ride, but in the off-season, only two or three trips a day were on the schedule.

As we spent several hours visiting both the old cathedral and the new, we saw many reminders of the devastation but also signs of the spirit of faith which made the people of Coventry vow to rise above the destruction. We felt their spirit was also akin to the true spirit of Christmas.

We learned that the very next morning after the bombing, November 15, 1940, the Reverend Dick Howard, the cathedral provost or administrator, announced the decision to rebuild. This was with the resolve that "rebuilding would not be an act of defiance, but rather a sign of faith, trust and hope for the future of the world."[1]

A few weeks after the Nazi attack on Coventry, Provost Howard on Christmas Day 1940 went on national radio from the cathedral ruins. He declared that when the war ended, he would work with England's former enemies "to build a kinder, more Christ-like world."

It would be nearly five years before the war ended in 1945, but the determination was firm. Replacing a cathedral is no small task, so it was more than a decade after the war when the foundation stone was laid in 1956. It was another six years before the new edifice was consecrated in May 1962, with Queen Elizabeth II, the official head of the Church of England, in attendance.

The walls of the old cathedral were left standing after the bombing, and they are still in place today along with the bell tower. The remains of that building, known as the Medieval Parish Church Cathedral of St Michael, and the modern Coventry Cathedral, also named for St Michael, are in close proximity, bringing together past and present.

As I walked in space which prior to 1940 had held hundreds of worshipers, I thought of a similar ghost-like roofless structure in Wales. While the Coventry cathedral had been destroyed by enemies from another country, the destroyers of Tintern Abbey and its accompanying monastery came from within: King Henry VIII broke with the Roman Catholic Church when Pope Clement VII refused to grant him a divorce. Subsequently, he started his own church, disbanded the convents and monasteries, and systematically destroyed many Catholic buildings, including those at Tintern on the Wye River.

In the historic Coventry cathedral, a vivid testimony of faith and reconciliation stands in the chancel area. On the wall behind the altar of the ruined building, the words "Father Forgive" are inscribed in gold lettering. Provost Howard authorized the inscription soon after the 1940 bombing. As cleanup was underway in the days following the attack, the cathedral's stonemason, Jock Forbes, noticed two large, charred roof timbers which had fallen in the shape of a cross. They were set up as a cross just behind the altar and in front of the "Father Forgive" inscription.

In keeping with Mr. Howard's commitment to work with Britain's enemies to make a Christ-like world, the "Coventry Litany of Reconciliation" was developed. The Litany is now prayed every weekday at noon in the new cathedral and in the Ruins on Fridays. A signboard bearing the Litany stands in front of the altar in the Ruins. It reads as follows:

"The Litany of Reconciliation"

"All have sinned and fallen short of the glory of God.

"The hatred which divides nation from nation, race from race, class from class,

Father Forgive.

"The covetous desires of people and nations to possess what is not their own,

Father Forgive.

"The greed which exploits the work of human hands and lays waste the earth,

Father Forgive.

"Our envy of the welfare and happiness of others,

Father Forgive.

"Our indifference to the plight of the imprisoned, the homeless, the refugee,

Father Forgive.

"The lust which dishonours the bodies of men, women and children,

Father Forgive.

"The pride which leads us to trust in ourselves and not in God,

Father Forgive.

"Be kind to one another, tender-hearted, forgiving one another, as God in Christ Forgave You."

In addition to Coventry there are two significant sites as tokens of reconciliation with former enemy nations: one in the historic cathedral for Japan and one in the new cathedral for Germany.

A sculpture in the old cathedral depicts kneeling figures, a man and a woman, leaning together in an embrace. A plaque on the base of the sculpture titled, "Reconciliation," has this inscription in English and Japanese:

"In 1995, 50 years after the end of the Second World War, this sculpture by Josefina de Vasconcellos has been given by Richard Branson as a token of reconciliation.

"An identical sculpture has been placed on behalf of the people of Coventry in the Peace Garden, Hiroshima, Japan.

"Both sculptures remind us that, in the face of destructive forces, human dignity and love will triumph over disaster and bring nations together in respect and peace."

The original version of the work showed the man and woman embracing across barbed wire.

It is reported that castings of this statue have also been placed in Berlin, Germany; and Belfast, Ireland, both as reminders of nations with internal warfare.

In the new cathedral, a bell mounted on a wall, has an accompanying plaque which reads, "This Bell inscribed in English and German with the word 'Peace' 'Friede' was presented to her Majesty Queen Elizabeth the Queen Mother by Richard Von Wiesacker, President of the Federal Republic of Germany during the service of reconciliation on the 50th Anniversary of the bombing of Coventry November 14th 1990."

Along with the wooden cross, a "cross of nails" was made from three large nails found in the wreckage. This cross of nails eventually was incorporated in a larger sculpture which stands on the altar in the new cathedral. Similar crosses of nails have been sent to other locations, including the German cities of Dresden, Kiel and Berlin, where major church buildings had been destroyed by allied forces.

With the urgent desire to continue a ministry of reconciliation, more than one hundred sixty local groups known as the Community of the Cross of Nails have formed in some sixty different nations, based on the cross of nails which originated in Coventry. The Litany of Reconciliation is also used by these groups.

A passage from Second Corinthians is the biblical basis for the ministry of reconciliation:

> *All this is from God, who through Christ reconciled us to himself and gave us the ministry of reconciliation; that is, in Christ God was reconciling the world to himself, not counting their trespasses against them, and entrusting to us the message of reconciliation. So we are ambassadors for Christ, God making his appeal through us. We beseech you on behalf of Christ, be reconciled to God. For our sake he made him to be sin who knew no sin, so that in him we might become the righteousness of God* (5:18-20).

In the aftermath of war, when a nation is seeking to get back on its feet after being bombarded, it's not the easiest thing to reach out in love and forgiveness to those who did the bombing. But the Christian leaders in Coventry set about to do that very thing.

The Coventry Christians realized they could not hope to succeed in reconciling their former attackers to God unless they themselves first sought to be reconciled to those attackers.

Christ, the central figure in reconciliation, is depicted in two statues in the old cathedral:

The "Ecce Homo" statue represents Christ before Pilate. His hands are bound, and a crown of thorns is on His head. The title is Latin for Pilate's words to the crowd: "Behold the man."

The other statue, with a halo and with hands extended, shows Christ blessing the multitudes.

The new cathedral is a magnificent structure. Its modern design included crucifixes, several large metal representations of the crown of thorns, and leaded glass windows. I confess that, over all, I found the remains of the historic St. Michael's more emotionally gripping.

Most compelling for me in the modern cathedral were six stained glass windows in the Chapel of Christ the Servant, one of several chapels in the cathedral complex. At first, these windows seemed strange, fragmentary. Upon closer examination, I realized three of them were angels and three others indeed were fragmentary by design.

The three angel panels are recreated sections of a chancel window. The 15th century glass in these windows was painted by John Thornton of Coventry, who also painted windows in other cathedrals.

The other three, known as "Medley" windows, are also from the chancel of the historic cathedral. Each of these windows has two or three faces, or partial faces, of people and angels, amid blocks of assorted colors and lettering. These montages are composed of unrelated pieces of stained glass.

I had assumed this glass was damaged during the 1940 air raid, but I learned later that the chancel windows were removed for safety before the war broke out. This was a common practice in major churches and cathedrals as war began to seem inevitable. After the cathedral was destroyed in the blitz, it was not possible to return the glass to the building. [2]

To me, there is deep symbolism in these glass panels being taken apart and then put back to form different images. In time of war, the nation was taken apart and then put back together in new patterns, not quite the same as before the war. Likewise, many individual men and women find their lives taken apart but, through reconciliation with Christ, are restored to new patterns of life.

As I began to understand what was going on in the Coventry Cathedrals, old and new, with emphasis on reconciliation and new life, the Christmas season seemed an especially significant time to visit this historic site.

The message of reconciliation is, in reality, the message of Christmas: *in Christ God was reconciling the world to himself, not counting their trespasses against them, and entrusting to us the message of reconciliation.*

Jesus came to the world to bring us back to His Father, and, we have been assigned the message of reconciliation.

---

[1] http://www.coventrycathedral.org.uk/about-us/our-reconciliation-ministry/the-community-of-the-cross-of-nails.php

[2] "A rare glimpse of unseen cathedral stained glass," http://www.bbc.co.uk/coventry/culture/stories/2002/08/cathedral-stained-glass.shtml

Caesar Aw-Gustus

"And it came to pass in those days that there went out a decree from Caesar Augustus that all the world should be taxed..."

As I was growing up in West Texas, I had heard and read Luke's Christmas story so often, I could quote from memory that opening verse and the entire story of the shepherds' visit to the manger.

Nobody had ever questioned my pronunciation of anything in that passage as I read it out loud from time to time while I was in high school, college, or seminary. But then, there was my first Christmas in my first church after seminary.

I had come to Pope Drive Baptist Church in Anderson, South Carolina, a few weeks before Christmas 1959 as a co-minister with multiple assignments. As a young, single minister, I spent a good bit of time with young people from the very beginning.

The morning service on the Sunday before Christmas was devoted to a program of music by the choir, interspersed with Scripture readings. On this, my first Christmas with the church, I was given the reading assignment.

I began reading Luke 2, with my West Texas pronunciation. That included pronouncing the emperor's title as Caesar "AW-gustus." This was natural for me, as someone born in August, who had heard that pronunciation all my life.

That handling – or mishandling – of the name doubtlessly brought smiles to the faces of adults in the congregation, but the teenagers didn't stop with smiles. They guffawed as I tried to continue the narration.

After the service, the youngsters mobbed me, peppering me with questions and teasing as they sought to set me straight on the way to say the word:

"Is that the way y'all talk out in Texas?"

"Haven't you ever heard of uh-GUST-uh, Georgia?"

"You're the minister of education? We need to educate you!"

And educate, they did – the kids and their parents during my four years with them.

The church was experiencing growing pains. The founding pastor, George Roberson, had the reputation among other ministers as the most persistent pastoral visitor in town, especially at the local hospital. When he started the church, he initially refused to take any money. Instead, he and his wife eked out an existence on her salary as a public school teacher. As an additional money-saving step, he and other men in the congregation had worked alongside local contractors in erecting the first unit of the church building. That first unit is now the Roberson Memorial Chapel.

In those early years, with "Preacher" Roberson's constant

visitation and the construction work in the neighborhood location, the church attracted attention and began to grow. So church lay leaders saw the need for a second minister to take care of aspects beyond the lead pastor's favorite focus. That's where I came in.

I did make visits to homes and the hospital, though I did not attempt to duplicate Mr. Roberson's day-in, day-out schedule.

I was the only paid worker besides the pastor and the janitor, and at times I helped both of them. Our choir was directed by a layman who refused to accept pay. We may have paid the high school girl who played the organ five dollars a week. I was variously perceived as minister of education, associate pastor, youth worker, assistant song leader, phone answerer, and typist. Two single young women volunteered their services to type the stencil for the Sunday order of worship and run off copies on the Mimeograph machine. My job description was basically, "Help Preacher Roberson and help us."

In retrospect, I think of how I helped raise a generation of young people, and their parents helped raise me. When I came to the church, I didn't own a car and didn't even have a driver's license. Two men in the congregation put their lives at risk as they rode with me in preparing me for the road test. No doubt, the prayer life of those parents increased exponentially when their teenagers started riding with me.

Baptists in the South in the 1960s had a multiplicity of educational organizations: Sunday school on Sunday morning and Training Union on Sunday night which sought to strengthen awareness of Baptist beliefs and traditions. Brotherhood for men and the Woman's Missionary Union had age-level auxiliaries for children and young people. As minister of education or "educational director," I planned and led various leadership training sessions on how to understand the Bible and how to break away from the lecture method in Sunday school; led weekday Bible studies for women who were not employed outside the home; and worked cooperatively with other churches in leadership training sessions.

When John F. Kennedy became the Democratic nominee for president in 1960, many Baptists were concerned about the implications of a Roman Catholic in the White House, fearful that President John might install a hot line to Pope John at the Vatican. So, at the request of some church members, we spent several Wednesday night sessions studying Catholic beliefs as objectively as Baptists of that era could do on our own. It didn't occur to us to invite a local priest or articulate lay member to give the Catholic perspective.

With young people, I planned times of food, games, and informal fellowship after the Sunday night service, often in homes of members. I planned recreational outings, took them to summer camp, and tailored various church meetings to their needs and interests.

Though I was an ordained minister and had studied to be a pastor-preacher, Mr. Roberson was not inclined to share his pulpit. In my four years with the church, I preached four times, including my final Sunday night with the congregation before I joined the faculty at Anderson College (now Anderson University).

Though it sounds like a cliché, the folks at Pope Drive accepted me into their homes and into their hearts. That is an understatement. I was often invited to Sunday dinner with various families, and there were several families where I often dropped by on week nights to share whatever fare, light or lavish, they were having. Deep bonds were formed which have lasted across the decades since I left their church.

After my four years at the church, I also spent four years at the college. While I was at the college, Pansy and I married. Then our path took various turns through several states before I was invited to return to the faculty in 1981. So we came back to Anderson and have continued to make this our home after we both retired in 2000.

With the concepts of ministerial ethics I had learned in college and seminary, when I ended my formal association with the church, I basically sought to end any regular contact with the church. But that did not mean I terminated my friendship with the many people who had ministered to me as I sought to be one of their ministers. It was and still is natural to have occasional contact with many of these dear friends who nurtured me in my beginning years of ministry. In those contacts, I have made it a point not to discuss internal affairs at the church.

Over the years, I have returned to Pope Drive occasionally to perform weddings and have frequently been called on to be one of the ministers for funerals. Most of these funerals in recent years have been for people in their eighties and nineties whom I had first known when they were middle-aged men and women, truly the "backbone of the church."

When Pansy and I left Anderson, I never dreamed I would have opportunity to return to this town, to teach again at the college and to be reunited with so many wonderful friends in the community at large and at Pope Drive. But people in the congregation were never far from my memory.

My pronunciation gaff in the Christmas program at Pope

Drive stands out as one clear memory, but in the four years with the church, I never actually spent Christmas Eve or Christmas Day in Anderson. The church was gracious in expecting and encouraging me, as a young, single man far from home, to go back to Texas to be with my parents and brothers and sisters and the extended Webb family.

The church gave me lasting Christmas gifts: loads of love and patience, right from that very first Christmas when I learned to pronounce Caesar Augustus, South Carolina style.

All I Hear is Germs and Jesus

TRUE STORY: A BOY IN THE SECOND GRADE was a Methodist preacher's son. The boy's mother was like most mothers in wanting her son to stay clean and healthy. One rainy day, the boy came in for supper, covered in mud. His mother told him to take a bath, warning him, as she often did, that he was likely to pick up germs when he played outside in the dirt. Because he had heard this so often, he blurted out, "All I ever hear in this house is germs and Jesus."

Here's another supposedly true story. A Sunday school teacher had planned a lesson about seeing God in nature. So he began by asking, "What is it that lives in trees, eats nuts, and has a long bushy tail?" One of the boys spoke up: "Well, it sounds like a squirrel. But since we're in church, it must be Jesus."

Children may wonder why all the talk in church is about Jesus. But Jesus really is – or should be – the main subject for Christian teaching and preaching, most especially at Christmas. So the boy hearing the squirrel story may have been on the right track after all: "Since we're in church, it must be Jesus." Or, to paraphrase, "Since we're at Christmas, it must be Jesus."

The whole New Testament never gets far away from Jesus, and, of all the books beyond the Gospels, the little letter called First John probably has more about Jesus per square inch than most others.

First John tells the Christmas story, but that story is told in a distinctive way. There are no shepherds, no angels, no Wise Men; not even Mary and Joseph make an appearance. But Jesus is there in the opening verses as the very Son of God, one the first readers had known intimately. They had heard Him. They had seen Him. They had physical contact with Him:

> *That which was from the beginning, which we have heard, which we have seen with our eyes, which we have looked upon and touched with our hands, concerning the word of life -- the life was made manifest, and we saw it, and testify to it, and proclaim to you the eternal life which was with the Father and was made manifest to us -- that which we have seen and heard we proclaim also to you, so that you may have fellowship with us; and our fellowship is with the Father and with his Son Jesus Christ* (1 John 1:1-3).

To say "Jesus is the Christ" is a way of saying Jesus was truly a man among men. John feels it necessary to emphasize the full humanity of Jesus -- a man with a physical body, like that of other men -- because there were teachers who said Jesus was an apparition, not an actual man. The word *Christ* is the Greek equivalent of the Hebrew word *Messiah* or Deliver. The Jews were looking for a Messiah, a man who would be their deliverer.

They were hoping for a military and political leader to deliver them from the domination of the Roman Empire. So they weren't prepared for the kind of Messiah Jesus turned out to be. But, again, when John stresses that Jesus is the Christ, this means Jesus is a man, The Man they have been looking for. Not some ethereal spirit but rather, flesh and blood. That's what John means when he says you are a child of God if you believe Jesus is the Christ.

But, alongside that emphasis on Jesus as a man, First John in chapter 5 also lays heavy emphasis on Jesus as the Son of God. In that final chapter, John calls Jesus the Son of God *nine times.* Nine times. In those nine references, he is saying this Man among men is also the very Son of God.

If you've raised children or worked with children at school or church or on sports teams or in other settings, you know you usually have to tell them something more than once to be sure they hear what you want them to hear. For that matter, you often have to repeat yourself with adults. Educators say repetition is a valuable form of teaching. If you go over something several times, it's more likely to be remembered. So if John seems repetitious, it's because he wants to be sure his readers understand and obey his instructions about Jesus. John probably would say, "It can't be said too often that Jesus is the Son of God."

This is beyond human understanding. It involves a leap of faith. When our grandson, Ethan, was eight years old, he broke a major supporting bone in his foot. He took a leap off a piece of playground equipment which was seven or eight feet tall. He wound up on crutches and then graduated to a medical apparatus called a boot which enabled him to walk without putting pressure on his broken foot. Lots of children jump off high places, but the better way, the safer way, is to jump into the arms of a parent. That is a leap of faith, the confidence that Mother or Daddy will catch them.

In adult life, we face adult-sized dangers, perhaps comparable to a child's false step which leads to a broken limb. Those adult dangers may be loss of a job which leads to loss of a house. Or loss of a significant life relationship through death or divorce or desertion. We may put ourselves in harm's way, spiritually, through wrong moral choices. Whatever form those dangers take, John says, *For whatever is born of God overcomes the world; and this is the victory that overcomes the world, our faith. Who is it that overcomes the world but he who believes that Jesus is the Son of God?*

Once again, it's all about Jesus. And we shouldn't get far away from Jesus Christ as we plan the holiday which bears His name.

John was especially concerned about some teachers who taught that Jesus was not truly a man. These teachers had been in the church, teaching against Jesus as the Christ. Because they were *against* Christ, John called them Anti-Christs.

[We need to detour from the Christmas story long enough to explain how the Bible uses the word Antichrist. The ONLY times Antichrist or Antichrists are mentioned in the Bible at all are in First John and its short, short companion, Second John. You can check these passages: First John 2:18–22 and 4:3; and Second John, verse 7. There is absolutely nothing in the Bible to connect these false teachers with the wooly booger Antichrist in fanciful novels and movies and unbiblical sermons. That villain is the product of

someone's fertile imagination.]

There were false teachers in that first Christian century who sought to detract from the wonderful story of Christmas as they declared Jesus was not the Christ, the promised Messiah. There have probably been similar false teachers in every generation. They are on the scene in our time. So we need those nine reminders from First John that Jesus Christ is the Son of God. The final two reminders come in 5:20--

> *And we know that the Son of God has come and has given us understanding, to know him who is true; and we are in him who is true, in his Son Jesus Christ. This is the true God and eternal life* [capitalizations added].

That verse would be a good place to end the letter of First John. But there is one more verse which isn't a nice, smooth way to end. Even so, we need this jarring reminder at Christmas:
Little children, keep yourselves from idols.
John isn't talking to actual little children who play in the mud. Scholars think the writer is an old man who has been the spiritual teacher and guide to the adults who first read the letter. They are dear to him, and he thinks of them as his children in the faith.

Some people in those days picked up more serious "germs" as they actually offered sacrifices at altars to gods of wood and stone. We are too sophisticated for that. But we have our own, more subtle, idols: bigger houses, bigger cars, boats, RVs, job promotions, and the list could go on.

We may idolize gifts under the tree: the latest in wireless

phones, new portable computers with ever-new programs to connect us with the latest music or words from our friends.

It may be difficult for us to turn away from the mud and germs of these inanimate gods which are pulsing with promise of thrills and more comfortable lifestyle.

But the call at Christmas in the twenty-first century is as necessary as it was in the first Century: *Keep yourselves from idols.*

Cecil Frances Alexander, the Irish lady who wrote the Christmas carol, "Once in Royal David's City," also wrote these words in the hymn, "Jesus Calls Us":

> *Jesus calls us from the worship*
> *Of the vain world's golden store,*
> *From each idol that would keep us,*
> *Saying, "Christian, love Me more!"*

---

* *The Methodist Hymnal.* Nashville, Tenn.: The United Methodist Publishing House, 1964, 1966, p. 107.

A Three-Inch Tall Jesus

When I was about twelve years old, the Sears, Roebuck store in Sweetwater had a Christmas shopping display which featured a real-live Santa Claus who was just three inches tall.

He lived in a tiny, but attractive, house which sat on a table. You could look in through the picture window and see the little man whom the store called Kute Kris Kringle. He was sitting by the fireplace in his easy chair in his living room which was decorated for the holidays with a tree and other greenery and with packages under the tree.

At times, this Tom Thumb-sized Santa would get up and walk around the room. He would look out and wave at those who watched him.

The most exciting thing about this was the tiny telephone on a table by his chair. It was connected with a full-sized phone on the table near the tiny gift bringer's house where customers watched him. If you wanted to talk with him, you could pick up the receiver and tell him what to bring you.

Parents would lead their kiddos to the display, point to the picture window, and get them to wave. If the little folks were brave, they could pick up the phone and tell the Jolly Little Elf their hearts' desires.

Because I had parted company with Old Saint Nick a few years earlier, I stood and watched, trying to figure how Sears, Roebuck managed to set up the display and get the real-live man to look so small.

Television was still a dream in West Texas in the mid-1940s, so I doubted that Sears had a television studio set up in some remote corner of the store.

After a while, I noticed a walled-off section immediately behind Kris Kingle's Little House on the Table and wondered why I hadn't seen it sooner. So I figured the full-grown man was just on the other side of that wall on a full-sized movie set which looked like a living room. My guess was that the illusion was made possible by using the principle of looking through the "wrong end" of a telescope.

With the boldness of late preadolescence, I picked up the phone one day to talk to Santa. That was OK with him . . . the first time. When I left the area and came back and called him several more times, the big man behind the three-inch illusion strongly suggested into his mouthpiece that I find something else to occupy my attention. I should leave the phone line open for younger boys and girls.

As I think back to how the Sears people had managed to shrink Santa Claus to a manageable size, it occurs to me that we try to do the same thing with Jesus. A three-inch tall Savior is much more convenient than the full-grown One who comes to life on the pages of the New Testament.

The Babe in Bethlehem with shepherds and angels and

Three Kings are a beautiful scene on our Christmas cards. If we have a creche on a table top in our family room, the stable is a bit larger than the Sears house where Santa lived, and the adult figures are considerably taller than three inches. But the Babe in the table-top manger may be just about three inches long. For added convenience, there are tree ornament versions of the manger scene, with the cattle stall and the figures in it, all reduced to no more than three inches. So there are various ways to keep the whole scene small enough not to be much bother. Then, too, when the season is over, we can pack them all up and get them out of our way without great inconvenience.

There are other ways – more serious ways – of keeping Jesus small beyond confining Him to the creche at Christmas.

Some people shrink Jesus to manageable size by saying He was a great teacher whose words are recorded in the Four Gospels. Nothing more. His homespun stories teach lessons everyone can benefit from. Some say, "The Sermon on the Mount is my guide for life," and that is the extent of their understanding about Jesus.

For those who claim to follow the Sermon on the Mount, one must wonder how they deal with these instructions: when someone strikes you on one side of the face, turn the other cheek; when someone tries to take away your coat, give him your overcoat as well; when you are compelled to walk a mile with someone, walk a second mile willingly.

Another way to bring Jesus down to size is to deny that He performed miracles. For example, when He appeared to be walking on the water, the disciples' boat was actually at the shore, and there was nothing mysterious about Jesus taking a few steps over to the vessel. Or when we are told of feeding a crowd of several thousand people with a few pieces of bread and fish, here's what they say really happened: He shamed the crowd into admitting they had brought food with them for the day's outing, so they took out their hidden food and shared with one another -- sort of an outdoor covered-dish luncheon.

In the case of miraculous cures, the Jesus shrinkers say He was a great psychologist who used strong power of suggestion to help people recover from psychosomatic ailments, nothing more.

When it comes to the New Testament's greatest miracle of all, the resurrection of Jesus, some modern interpreters say those original followers wanted so badly for Him to come back to them that they believed He actually was raised from the dead. But it makes little sense to suggest mere daydreams or wishful thinking could have given the original impetus which caused the small, insignificant movement to catch fire and grow, even in the face of persecution, imprisonment, and death. Likewise, if the resurrection was a delusion, how do we explain the millions of people across the centuries whose lives have been transformed through faith in a fairy tale? The course of Christianity history cannot be so handily dismissed.

Some people simply dismiss the entire Bible out of hand or rewrite it to suit themselves. President Thomas Jefferson published his own version of the Bible which basically contained Jesus' teaching but none of the miracles. The Jefferson Bible ends with the corpse being buried.

As we consider these and other ways people try to shrink Jesus to fit their own specifications, we acknowledge the stories in the Bible are not based on scientific evidence. It takes the eye of faith to see Jesus as more than a great teacher, more than a healer of diseases of the mind, as the One who rose from the dead and brings everlasting life.

Faith and science need not be seen as mortal enemies. Many scientists are devout followers of Christ who believe, for example, that God used the evolutionary process to bring about life on earth, over millions of years, beginning with the simplest one-celled animals and developing all the way to human beings. These scientists do not believe Jesus must be shrunk in size in order for us to see the validity of the scientific process.

Science is based on measurable evidence which can be evaluated under the microscope or in laboratory or field experiments. Christian claims regarding the person of Jesus and the wonders ascribed for Him in the New Testament belong to a past age and cannot be replicated. But this does not mean they did not happen.

The world has been blessed by countless wonders of science. In our technological era, we rely on science every day, at every turn, for our health, transportation, communication, and entertainment. So followers of Jesus can ill afford to dismiss science. Neither should scientists attempt to dismiss the realm of faith which lies beyond scientific proof.

Regarding the world and how it got here, Christians should respect science as it explains HOW it all happened, and scientists should respect those in the faith community who explain WHO made it happen. They need not be at war.

Albert Einstein, often considered one of the most brilliant persons who ever lived, said he did not believe in a personal God and referred to himself as agnostic, but he was not openly antagonistic toward religious faith.

Currently, famous atheists such as Richard Dawkins and

Christopher Hitchens are evangelistic against religious faith as they seek to reduce Jesus to absolute zero. But I have fewer problems with avowed atheists or agnostics than professing Christians, who seek to whittle Jesus down to size in ways suggested earlier in this essay. I have heard internationally famous Bible professors state categorically that certain incidents reported in the Bible simply did not happen, could not have happened. They offer no evidence to support their assertions. They simply deny these things as being possible.

Also, several years ago, a group of scholars formed what is known as the Jesus Seminar. Their self-assigned task was to analyze all the sayings attributed to Jesus in the Four Gospels to determine which sayings are authentic and which are not. By their own authority, they grouped the sayings according to whether they are authentic, questionable, or definitely not from Jesus. They declared, for example, that the Fourth Gospel, contains no authentic words from Jesus. By their reckoning, the entire book was composed by the church in a later generation, with no sayings which can be traced back to Jesus. This approach doesn't even leave Jesus three inches tall.

To my thinking, the most significant bona fide whittling down of Jesus is described in the Christmas Story as told by St. Paul in the second chapter of Philippians. He describes Jesus as being in *the form of God* but not clinging to that closeness to God the Father. Rather, Jesus did His own whittling as He *"emptied himself, taking the form of a servant, being born in the likeness of men. And being found in human form he humbled himself and became obedient unto death, even death on a cross"* (Philippians 2:6-8).

Charles Wesley, one of Methodism's founding brothers, in

his song, "And Can It Be," described Jesus's willingness to lay aside His heavenly perks:

He left His Father's throne above So free, so infinite His grace — Emptied Himself *of all but love, And bled for Adam's helpless race.**

But the Jesus in the Bible Story did not remain in the grave and did not remain in the whittled-down form. Instead, God the Father restored Him to His full stature:

"Therefore God has highly exalted him and bestowed on him the name which is above every name, that at the name of Jesus every knee should bow, in heaven and on earth and under the earth, and every tongue confess that Jesus Christ is Lord to the glory of God the Father" (Philippians 2:9-11).

No three-inch Jesus here!

---

* Charles Wesley, "And Can It Be," *The Baptist Hymnal.* Nashville, Tenn.: Convention Press, 1991, p. 147.

The Gift of the Magi

SOME PEOPLE SAY, "WE WERE POOR when we were growing up, but we didn't *know* we were poor."

Those who say this probably grew up during the Great Depression of the 1930s. All their neighbors faced the problem of trying to scrape up enough money to cover absolute necessities, so there was little class consciousness among them. Now Depression survivors look back, and those early years have a golden glow as they recall loving parents who softened the pain of poverty.

But Della Young, the wife in O. Henry's short story, "The Gift of the Magi," knew very well that she was poor.

In the story set in the first decade of the 20th century, Della's husband Jim's weekly pay had shrunk from thirty dollars a week to twenty dollars, and rent for their walk-up flat took eight dollars of that. So times were rough.

Della wanted so badly to get a special Christmas gift for Jim. His prize possession – other than Della – was a handsome gold pocket watch. It had been passed down from Jim's grandfather and father. That magnificent watch had no chain, but simply a plain leather strap to connect the watch in the watch pocket to a belt loop. With the unattractive leather strap, Jim, perhaps a bit self-consciously, pulled his prized watch from its pocket many times a day to check the time. So Della was determined to find a way to buy a platinum chain to set off the watch appropriately.

She knew the chain she wanted for her Jim's watch would cost many dollars, and she had the grand total of one dollar and eighty-seven cents. That scant amount had come as she almost literally pinched pennies, one or two at a time through frugal shopping at the grocer and the butcher shop. But it was Christmas Eve, and she had no means of spanning the gap between her dollar eighty-seven and the huge price ticket she knew she would find on the chain.

One of the most striking aspects of Della's beauty was her flowing brown hair which reached below her knees and swaddled her like a robe. Jim adored her hair, and he was determined to buy a set of combs which would go well with her hair. He and she had seen the combs in a store window. They were made of pure tortoise shell with jeweled rims, and he hoped to buy them as her Christmas present.

Della sat on the furnished sofa in their furnished flat on that Christmas Eve with tears coursing down her pretty young face. Then she wiped away her tears as she remembered a store window sign which might hold the key to her dilemma.

She put on her jacket and her hat, then hurried down the stairs and into the street, hardly slowing until she found the store with the sign which read, "Hair goods of all kinds." Determined not to lose a minute, Della rushed into the salon and asked the proprietor whether she bought hair. When she heard the affirmative answer and learned she could get twenty dollars, she agreed to the woman's price and asked that the work be done quickly.

With very short hair on her head and the sum of twenty-one dollars and eighty-seven cents as her entire fortune, Della continued her race against time. Stores would soon be closing for Christmas. With the sense that time was running out, she searched through several stores before finding the special chain for Jim's extra special watch. The chain cost exactly twenty-one dollars, so she headed back to the flat with one platinum chain and eighty-seven cents.

Back in the flat, the race continued. She had to heat her curling irons and turn the remains of her long hair into short curls before she would hear Jim's fast steps on the stairs. Even so, she dreaded his reaction to the loss of her long brown hair, which she knew he admired deeply. She hoped the sight of his new chain would ease the shock, and she prayed Jim would still think she was pretty.

When Jim entered their flat, he stared at Della in total unbelief and muttered over and over about her missing hair. She explained how she had sold her hair in order to buy him a present he would appreciate.

Jim took his surprise present from his coat, tossed the package on the table, and told Della to open it. She gasped in amazement as she saw the combs, then tried to assure Jim that her hair would grow back quickly. Then she showed Jim the chain and asked him to let her attach it to his watch. At that point, Jim had to confess he had sold his watch in order to buy the combs for Della.

For O. Henry, whose pen name is synonymous with surprise endings, this story is Exhibit A.

In a post script to this tale, the author points to the biblical magi: "wonderfully wise men--who brought gifts to the Babe in the manger." He credits these men with inventing "the art of giving Christmas presents" and says, "their gifts were no doubt wise ones." Then O. Henry, whose birth name was William Sydney Porter, speaks of Jim and Della as "foolish children . . . who most unwisely sacrificed for each other the greatest treasures of their house." But, then, paradoxically, he says these two are the wisest of all who give gifts. His final words regarding Della and Jim: "They are the magi." *

Perhaps the description of the young couple as foolish is offered with tongue in cheek: the evaluation we may readily give when we learn of sacrificial or extravagant gifts which others have made.

The magi from Matthew might also be judged foolish for spending weeks or months in travel, searching for a newborn King of the Jews – considered unwise for bringing lavish gifts which ultimately were laid at the feet of the child of ordinary working parents. Hindsight says they were foolish for misinterpreting the kind of king this baby was to be. But as they got back on track in following their star, they pointed the way for all who devote time, energy, and resources in search of a King for their lives.

Nothing in O. Henry's story is especially religious, other than the mention that Della had a habit of praying silently about simple, everyday matters. But everyday prayer is no small thing. Indeed, that habit of prayer apparently led her to sacrifice something meaningful to her for the sake of the one she loved the most.

When the story ends, we see an underlying love which does not depend on how much, or even whether, we give of material things. Della is minus her hair and Jim his watch, but they have something much more important: Each other.

If we genuinely love other people, we may feel led to make sacrifices for those in our families, in our circle of friends, and even those beyond our immediate associates when we recognize them as members of God's family.

The ultimate example of God's love gift is Jesus, whose birthday is celebrated by magi, ancient and modern.

Greater love hath no man than this, that a man lay down his life for his friends (John 15:13 KJV).

But God shows his own love for us in that while we were still sinners, Christ died for us (Romans 5:8).

"Thanks be to God for His inexpressible gift" (2 Corinthians 9:15).

---

* O. Henry, "The Gift of the Magi," Project Gutenberg, http://www.gutenberg.org/catalog/world/readfile?fk_files=1466378

Look at That Star

A CHRISTMAS SPIRITUAL HAS RECLAIMED my attention. Its recurring theme: "Look-a that star shine in the night, showin' the way to Bethlehem."

Several other songs about the Star of Bethlehem readily come to mind. But this one has especially worked its way into my mind and heart.

The song is on a CD we bought several years ago when we visited the historic Ephrata Cloister in Ephrata, Pennsylvania. This Protestant religious community, which admitted both celibate "brothers and sisters" and married families, existed approximately two centuries, ending in the 1930s. From its beginning, the Cloister was noted for its a cappella choral music, such as that on the CD, *Christmas at the Cloister*. [1]

From those early days, Ephrata had a printing press, and the community is thought to have printed the first Christmas card in America on that press. The card contained this verse of praise to Jesus:

No name is so beautiful as my Jesus' name,
While in German he is so often called Savior,
This child is also the true woman-seed,
Who alone shows us the way to everlasting life;
This name I will engrave deep in my heart,
And in my last need will have it in my mouth. [2]

When we got home from our trip to Pennsylvania, I lost little time loading the music on to our computers. Then I largely neglected the entire album until recently when I was browsing our iTunes listings.

The Ephrata Cloister Chorus's vibrancy and warmth which shine through their rich harmony particularly captivated me on "Look-a That Star."

The song actually is not an old Negro spiritual. Rather, it was written by a modern-day white composer, Jay Althouse.[3]

My fellow white-man ears have little formal music training. But I think the song catches the spirit of traditional black music, with its high energy and frequent repetition of the refrain: "Look-a that star shine in the night/ Showin' the way to Bethlehem."

In our minds, Bethlehem's star has come to symbolize all the light of Christmas. We may tend to think of the star as shining over the stable where Jesus was born or even as giving light to the shepherds in the fields. Luke 2 mentions no light at the stable, although it is reasonable to imagine Joseph improvised some kind of light for Mary as she gave birth to her Son. In the account of the angels appearing to the shepherds, we are told of God's glory shining around the men, but we are not told exactly what that might mean:

And an angel of the Lord appeared to them, and the glory of the Lord shone around them, and they were filled with fear (Luke 2:9).

In Scripture, the only time the Christmas star appears is when it guides the Wise Men from the East as they start their journey to find the newborn King of the Jews.

In our imagination, we might hear them sing as they travel, "Look-a that star shine in the night, showin' the way to Bethlehem."

When they are approaching Bethlehem, the Wise Men follow their own logic rather than the star. They draw the erroneous conclusion that the King of the Jews whom they seek will be born in the royal palace in the capital city of Jerusalem, not in the little village of Bethlehem nearby. So they take their eyes off the star which had been a reliable guide as it was "showin' the way to Bethlehem" (Matthew 2:1-2):

Now when Jesus was born in Bethlehem of Judea in the days of Herod the king, behold, wise men from the East came to Jerusalem, saying, "Where is he who has been born king of the Jews? For we have seen his star in the East, and have come to worship him."

The Wise Men feel less than wise when they realize King Herod wants to have this newborn King of the Jews put to death. So, they leave the palace and, once again, are able to sing, "Look-a that star":

When they had heard the king they went their way; and lo, the star which they had seen in the East went before them, till it came to rest over the place where the child was. When they saw the star, they rejoiced exceedingly with great joy (Matthew 2:9-10).

They realize the Christmas star did not leave them. They had turned away from it. Once again, the star is "showin' the way to Bethlehem," where they find the Baby and His parents (Matthew 2:11-12):

[A]nd going into the house they saw the child with Mary his mother, and they fell down and worshiped him. Then, opening their treasures, they offered him gifts, gold and frankincense and myrrh.

After the Wise Men find their King, they, wisely, return home another way, rather than repeating their mistake by returning to the palace:

And being warned in a dream not to return to Herod, they departed to their own country by another way (Matthew 2:12).

The Bible gives no precise identification of these men beyond the verses we've seen here. So we know little about the men or their star. In the Greek of the New Testament, they are called *Magi*, which means astrologers. So they likely were men who gave serious study to the movement of celestial bodies.

In centuries preceding the birth of Jesus, the expectation of a Messiah, or great deliverer, was found throughout the Middle

East. So these Wise Men may have been searching the night skies when they saw what they believed was their guiding star which would lead them to the newborn King of the Jews.

In modern times, Bible students have made various efforts to identify the specific star or constellation the Wise Men followed. Modern scholars have searched ancient records of unusual movements of stars and planets. But all these efforts have proven inconclusive. Astronomy offers no objective evidence to help us know just what the Wise Men's star was.

Christmas cards and other religious art often picture three men on camels riding in a circle of light from that star. Those scenes are based on assumptions, rather than on factual evidence. Tradition has transformed the Bible's unspecified number of Magi into three kings and given each man a name (Balthazar, Gaspar, and Melchior). But there is no biblical basis for this tradition. As for the pool of light the Three Kings ride in, it is more likely that the men, of whatever number, got their bearing by looking to the heavens, rather than by riding toward Bethlehem under a powerful ray of light which moved with them.

The Wise Men's ability to track their "star of wonder, star of night" may be roughly comparable to that of astronomers who followed the latest appearance of Halley's Comet in 1986. This comet, which goes across the skies approximately every seventy-five or seventy-six years, sometimes is accompanied by heavenly fireworks, readily seen by the naked eye. On one occasion, the comet was described as having a long tail like a dragon.

At times, the comet's anticipated arrival was thought to be a sure sign of the end of the world.

In the fifteenth century, the predicted arrival created such anxiety among the people that Pope Calixtus III excommunicated the comet as an agent of the devil. [4]

Halley's Comet, tracked for more than two thousand years, made an appearance in 12 B. C. Because we don't know the exact year of Jesus's birth, this date seemed close enough to the date for some Bible students to try to make Halley's the Wise Men's star. But, as with other efforts, this is another conjecture which cannot be proved.

Halley's 1986 appearance was greeted with much fanfare in our area. Astronomy professors set up telescopes in an open field and encouraged people to drop by and look at this phenomenon. Pansy and I went to the site but could see nothing with our unaided eyes. Even by peering through the telescopes, we saw nothing memorable to our untrained eyes. To my mind, the Star of Bethlehem, in similar fashion, required an eye which knew what to look for as it looked to the heavens. Matthew's Wise Men had eyes which could see what most people could not and did not not see. This enabled them to say, "Look-a that star shine in the night, showin' the way to Bethlehem."

It's good to have intellectual curiosity. But, finally, we must learn to walk by faith, not by sight (2 Corinthians 5:7) in matters spiritual. When we try to get specific, objective information beyond the Bible regarding details of the number of men and the exact nature of their star, could we be taking our eyes off the star, as our travelers did in search of the King?

The verse on that early Christmas card from the Ephrata Cloister has this assertion about Jesus:
It is He "Who alone shows us the way to everlasting life."

Our challenge is to follow the example of the Wise Men

at their wisest, keeping our eyes fixed on the heavens so we can point the way of faith, as we "Look-a that star shine in the night, showin' the way to Bethlehem."

---

[1] Purchase information: The *Christmas at the Cloister* CD was produced by Ephrata Cloister Associates in 2005. This CD and other music can be ordered online: www.ephratacloister.org/store.htm.

[2] The verse from the early Christmas card is quoted in the booklet accompanying the CD, *Christmas at the Cloister.*

[3] "Althouse, Jay L.," *Hope Hymnody Online,* www.hopepublishing.com/html/main.isx?sub=27&search=302

[4] Nick Greene, "Halley's Comet," *About.com.* http://space.about.com/od/comets/a/halleyscomet.htm

My First Christmas Memory

IN MY FIRST CLEAR MEMORY OF CHRISTMAS, I am riding a bus which is on its way to a church in a village south of Sweetwater, Texas.

This is also one of my very early memories, Christmas or otherwise. Lay leaders and one pastor in particular from that little Nolan Baptist Church would make a strong impact on me throughout my public school years.

In that early memory, we are living with Mother's mother in her little three-room house on her ninety-seven-acre farm. That is small acreage by standards of the farms and ranches in the Nolan-Divide community. Grandma's farm is four or five miles from the church.

The seats on the bus are padded and are all around the edges of the interior of the bus. There is open space in the center. Some of us boys and girls sit in that open space at our parents' feet.

[*Looking back to those Depression years, I imagine the church ran the bus out of consideration for the members and scarcity of money for gas for their cars.*]

The scene from long ago continues as we are in the church. I sit between Mother and Daddy as a Christmas program is in progress. A man and a woman are on the platform at the front. The woman is seated, holding a baby or maybe a doll. The man stands beside her.

There is singing. During one song, three men walk down the center aisle dressed in bath robes and holding shiny objects in their hands. They have crowns on their heads. The song is about kings. It has words that are hard for me to understand. [*That's about all I remember. This is in the late 1930s. I'm not sure whether this is my third or fourth Christmas.*]

I referred to this experience in my book, *Christmas Memories from Seven to Seventy.*[1] Though I remember little else about that Christmas, I have many memories of the Nolan Baptist Church across my childhood and youth.

We attended several different churches during my growing-up years as Daddy moved from farm job to farm job in two or three counties near Sweetwater. But we often returned to Grandma's farm. So I consider the Nolan Church my "home church" during most of my pre-college years.

Mrs. Ross Artman is one of several people in the Nolan Church who stand out in my memory. She was my Sunday school teacher in my first years of school. She was an elderly lady who told us Bible stories and taught us songs. I especially remember two songs. One song was "Let the Beauty of Jesus Be Seen in Me."[2] It referred to His "passion and purity" and included a prayer: "O Thou Spirit divine, all my nature refine."

Another song, "I Want to Live as Jesus Lived,"[3] said in part, "I want to serve and honor Him and please Him in everything."

Though I did not understand some of the words to these songs, I sensed a kind and gentle spirit in Mrs. Artman and felt I could see the beauty of Jesus in her. Also, I believed she wanted to please Jesus in everything she did.

Another adult who made a lasting impression a few years later was Hoyt Shelton. His daughter Marvell and I were in the same grade in school all through the years. Mr. Shelton worked with us on Sunday night in Baptist Training Union--BTU, we called it. On Sunday morning in Sunday school, teachers mostly stood at the front of the room and talked to us. But BTU was different:

The study material was divided into four or five "parts" to be presented to the group by different members of the group. Each part was no more than five or six short paragraphs. We took turns standing in front of our peers and "giving parts on program." In Training Union, we were also encouraged to do "Daily Bible Reading" at home during the week. Then, one of us was assigned to be the Bible Readers Leader and prepare a quiz based on the week's readings. I remember Hoyt Shelton gave me the job as Bible Readers Leader. In that role and in giving my part from week to week, I gained the confidence to stand before a group and speak. This practice would stand me in good stead in coming years.

[*Years later, I would write similar study materials, composed of four or five parts, used by teenagers in churches across the continent.*]

Each summer, the Nolan church would have a two-week revival meeting under a tent owned by the church. It would be set up on the church grounds, and all the pews and chairs from the building would be moved to the tent for the duration. In the summer of 1945, shortly before my eleventh birthday, I made my profession of faith in Christ during the "invitation hymn" at the end of a Sunday morning service of the revival. Several other boys, some about my age and some older, also made public professions of faith, and all of us were baptized in a community lake a mile or so from the church on the last Sunday afternoon of the meeting.

But I didn't "walk the aisle" under that revival tent because I saw Bill McDonald or Charles Bledsoe go forward and take the preacher's hand. Preparation for my public decision could be traced back to that early Christmas memory in that same little church---and even earlier. My mother and her mother instilled awareness of Jesus and His teachings in my brothers and sisters and me, so early in life that it would be impossible to look back and recall when it began.

Against that general backdrop, a specific moment came which made me aware of my need for a personal commitment of faith in Christ. A few months prior to that summer revival, my older sister, Leta, talked with my older brother, Lee Roy, and me one Sunday night while we were listening to a church service on the radio. From that time, I gave a great deal of thought about this as a need in my life. So that day of public decision and that moment in the lake at the end of a revival service were the culmination of years of godly influence from Mother and Grandma and the specific words of loving concern from my older sister a few months earlier.

That little Nolan Baptist Church was also the environment in which I first felt an inner urging that I interpreted as a "call to preach." This was met by an inner resistance. I was about fourteen when I first sensed this calling, but I kept it to myself for two to three years. Though I did not verbalize my struggle with anyone, I learned later that our pastor at Nolan sensed my struggle. Buren Higdon spent a lot of time with the teenagers in his church, encouraging us and listening to us. He and the lay leaders planned events for us, and he took time with us teenage boys, getting to know us on an informal basis.

Though Pastor Higdon and I never talked directly about the calling to ministry, he always took time to talk and listen when I showed up at church early on Wednesday night or Sunday night. He also loaned me books on religious subjects, including biographies of ministers.

He left our church a short time before I made my public announcement of intention to study for the ministry, but I saw him not long afterward and told him of my decision.

He surprised me by saying, "I didn't know you had made it public, but I knew you were struggling with that decision."

In response, I asked, "Why didn't you say something to me? A word from you would have been all it took for me to make it public."

He said, wisely, I think: "No. That had to be your decision, not mine. You had to come to that on your own. I didn't want people saying Buren Higdon called you to preach."

A few years later, I reconnected with this pastor who had been my silent sounding board. He was taking college courses while he was with the Nolan congregation. Then, when I enrolled at Hardin-Simmons University in Abilene, he was pastor of a church in town as he completed his degree. There, we shared classes, and I became comfortable calling him by his first name.

By the time I graduated from our little country school and went to Hardin-Simmons, our family had settled in Sweetwater, and we became members of Lamar Street Baptist Church there. So, without planning it that way, Nolan Baptist Church became part of my past. After graduation, the next time I was back at the church was some twelve years later in 1963 when Grandma died, and her funeral service was conducted there.

Soon after her death, we sold Grandma's farm, thus ending our physical connection with the Nolan-Divide community. In time, all of us, including Daddy and Mother, moved away from Sweetwater. I had moved farthest when I went to seminary in Kentucky and then spent most of my adult life in the Southeast.

After Grandma's funeral, I was not back in the church again until 2010 when Pansy and I were visiting my siblings a couple of hundred miles east of Sweetwater in Waco, Waxahachie, and Cleburne. When my younger brother Leonard learned we were planning to go to West Texas on that trip, he got in touch with Vic Meyer, the current pastor at Nolan, and asked if he would let me preach when we were in the area. Pastor Meyer graciously agreed, not realizing his small congregation would be flooded with a virtual army of Webb relatives.

As it turned out, all five surviving Webb siblings converged on the church on the day I preached. We were accompanied by most of the spouses and a cousin or two.

We drove by Grandma's farm, but the boundary lines between her land and adjoining farms had disappeared. Smaller farms had been merged into larger tracts of land under single ownership. So it was difficult to tell exactly where the house and barn had been. From the road, the only visible landmark was the windmill which had supplied our water for drinking, cooking, washing, and feeding the cows. That little windmill now is dwarfed by giant windmills all around: turbines which capture the wind to be used for energy.

At the church, we were received warmly on a windy, almost wintry March day. Women in the church prepared a covered dish lunch, and I enjoyed a reunion with several schoolmates I had not seen since I graduated.

Standing behind the pulpit that morning, I was among friends, old and new. I gave thanks for the many ways the Nolan Baptist Church had shaped my life in those formative years. Many memories rushed back as I stood on that same platform where the Christmas pageant unfolded more than seventy years before, with Mary and Joseph and the Baby at the front and the Three Kings marching down the aisle.

---

[1] *Christmas Memories from Seven to Seventy* is available through booksellers listed on the copyright page of this book.

[2] "Albert Orsbon, "Let the Beauty of Jesus Be Seen in Me," *Sanctum, Diverse Music for Choirs & Ensembles*, http://www.afsanctum.com/pages/sg500611"

[3] Albert Orsbon, "I Want to Live as Jesus Lived," *Sean Reagan*, http://seanreagan.com/let-the-beauty-of-jesus-be-seen-in-me/"

Once for a Shining Hour

IT'S JUST A FLAT, CLEAR, PLASTIC DISK about three inches in diameter, one of the plainest among our several hundred tree ornaments. It doesn't look like much. Still, it's one of my favorites. After all, as I remind myself when I stand before the mirror, looks aren't everything.

The design is simple: a star in the upper left-hand corner with rays extending outward. Nothing terribly compelling there.

So, it comes down to the nine words on the disk: "Once for a Shining Hour, Heaven Touched the Earth." That sentence may sound simple, but, on closer examination, its message is profound.

The statement has to do with what Christian theologians call the Incarnation: Jesus, who was one with God, became a real live person -- incarnated, which means "in the flesh." John 1 identifies Jesus as the Eternal Word from God: *And the Word became flesh* [incarnate] *and dwelt among us, full of grace and truth; we have beheld his glory, glory as of the only Son from the*

Father (1:14).

With that in mind, consider the key words on that plastic disk:

ONCE for a shining hour, heaven touched the earth.

Christians believe Jesus came as the unique, one-time, non-repeatable revelation of God's love for humanity.

When the time was right, St. Paul declared, God sent Jesus into the world:

> *But when the time had fully come, God sent forth his Son, born of woman, born under the law, to redeem those who were under the law, so that we might receive adoption as sons* (Galatians 4:4-5).

God doesn't operate on our time. God is concerned with our lives which are lived out in time, but God isn't bound by our understanding of time. God understands the long sweep of time and can see long-term implications of how we spend our time. All this was factored into God's judgment that the time was right for sending Jesus for that once-for-all event.

Once for a SHINING hour, heaven touched the earth.

We associate bright lights with Christmas. The twinkling lights on our trees can call to mind the light of the star which led the Wise Men (Matthew 2:1-2). Or they remind us of the light of the glory of God which shone around the shepherds when the angels came to tell them of the birth of the Savior

(Luke 2:9).

John says of the Word made flesh: *In him was life, and the life was the light of men. The light shines in the darkness, and the darkness has not overcome it* (John 1:4-5). Later in John, Jesus identifies Himself as light: *"I am the light of the world; he who follows me will not walk in darkness, but will have the light of life"* (John 8:12).

So, in that one bright shining instant, Jesus came to bring us to the light of God. That light continues to shine through people of faith into a spiritually darkened world.

Once for a shining HOUR, heaven touched the earth.

The reference to "a shining hour" points to the brevity of Jesus's time on earth from the perspective of eternity.

Psalm 90 contrasts time as seen by the Eternal God and as seen by a man. Compare the seventy or eighty years a person might expect to live with God's understanding of time; *For a thousand years in thy sight are but as yesterday when it is past, or as a watch in the night* (verse 4).

With that comparison, we might think of Jesus's thirty years or so on earth as about an hour. So, for that shining hour, Jesus directly touched the earth.

But let's reverse that comparison. Consider what one well-spent sixty-minute period -- one hour -- could mean over the span of a thousand years.

An hour spent carefully listening to and encouraging a child might be what it takes to start that boy or girl on a constructive path. As more hours are added in that mentoring relationship, that youngster could, in later years, enter a career in which he or she invests time and energy in the lives of others. Those people, in turn could be part of a never-ending stream of helpfulness, all because you or I spent an hour in a way that reflected the spirit of Christ, who spent His brief "hour" pouring out His love for others.

Howard Thurman in *The Mood of Christmas** has written similarly, how an impression may be made by someone who briefly touches a child's life and then moves on. He said this seemingly incidental contact may eventually touch millions of lives as that child becomes a national leader.

When my friend Everette Newman was growing up in West Virginia, he was a street kid, spending time around gangs. He readily says, if that had not changed, he might well have wasted his life. But someone who remained anonymous saw Everette on the streets and in the alleys and decided to point him in a new direction by giving him a scholarship to the local YMCA.

Coaches at the Y soon discovered Everette had a great talent for baseball and took personal interest in him. Everette's athletic ability enabled him to go to college on scholarship. He also played professional baseball and used his earnings to go to law school at the University of South Carolina.

Everette continues to have a strong interest in sports, attending games far and wide and encouraging young athletes, as he had been encouraged. He also follows the lead of that anonymous donor from his boyhood as an active member and major financial supporter of the YMCA in his adopted hometown.

His boyhood coaches at the Y in West Virginia invested many hours with him, but if we think symbolically of their time as an hour, there is no way to calculate the impact of that hour for years and decades to come. Their investment of time and energy with Everette is multiplied through his continuing influence on others. Perhaps that is a small example on the human level of the eternal impact of the "shining hour" Jesus spent on earth.

You, too, should consider the difference one hour could make if you spend it reaching out in love to someone in need this Christmas.

Once for a shining hour, HEAVEN touched the earth.

As the word is used on my Christmas decoration, heaven is an indirect, impersonal reference to the God of heaven, God who created the heavens and the earth. The ancient Jews held God in such high esteem that they refused even to speak the name of God. In reading aloud, they would use a substitute name or pass over the divine name all together. Perhaps the creator of this tree ornament had some of that same feeling, choosing the indirect reference to God.

God is Spirit and, thus, is not restricted to any geographic space. But we think of heaven as Up There. The psalmist used the height of heaven to show how God is exalted above the earth but still is like a father who accepts and forgives his children:

> *For as the heavens are high above the earth, so great is his steadfast love toward those who fear him; as far as the east is from the west, so far does he remove our transgressions from us. As a father pities his children, so the LORD pities those who fear him* (Psalm 103:11-13).

**Once for a shining hour,
heaven TOUCHED the earth.**

When the description on my Christmas ornament says, "Heaven touch the earth," this does not describe an astronomical collision. It's bigger, more dramatic, than that. This means God sent Jesus to earth, the physical representative of the "Very God of Very God," in the words of the Nicene Creed.

The God of heaven touched the earth in the process of bringing it into existence.

The God of heaven touched the earth as He created humankind in His own image.

The God of heaven touched the earth through spoken messages by the prophets.

We as Christians proclaim that the God of heaven touched the earth in a unique manner when Jesus was born in Bethlehem.

Jesus, the representative of heaven, came to our realm. He physically touched and occupied our space with us.

Through Jesus, the God of heaven touched the earth with His love, the love which ultimately led Jesus to give His life as a ransom for many (Mark 10:45).

When comets or planets come closer to our world than they normally do in their orbits, astronomers worry about possible disaster. But when "Heaven touched the earth" on that first Christmas, it was all positive, all for our benefit.

**Once for a shining hour,
heaven touched the EARTH**

We began by considering how Jesus, the Eternal Word, came to earth. Now consider how His coming to earth was for the purpose of loving and redeeming the residents of earth.

In the figurative language of Genesis 2, the human race is made from the earth:

Then the LORD God formed man of dust from the ground, and breathed into his nostrils the breath of life; and man became a living being (Genesis 2:7).

Genesis 1 says God created us in His own image: *So God created man in his own image, in the image of God he created him; male and female he created them* (Genesis 1:27).

As we think of the God of heaven touching the earth in the coming of Christ, the most wondrous aspect of that is in Romans 5:

But God shows his love for us in that while we were yet sinners Christ died for us. Since, therefore, we are now justified by his blood, much more shall we be saved by him from the wrath of God. For if while we were enemies we were reconciled to God by the death of his Son, much more, now that we are reconciled, shall we be saved by his life (Romans 5:8-10).

The purpose of heaven's touching the earth is summed up in John 3:16, The Christmas Story in a Sentence: *For God so loved the world that he gave his only Son, that whoever believes in him should not perish but have eternal life.*

All this and more comes to my mind as I reflect on that plain, simple, flat, clear, plastic disk. Each time, as I hold the ornament in my hand before I place it on our Christmas tree,

I think again on the implications of those words:
 "Once for a Shining Hour, Heaven Touched the Earth."

---

*Howard Thurman, *The Mood of Christmas.* Richmond, Indiana: Friends United Press, 1985. ©Howard Thurman, 1973.

Christmas Eve Gift

WHEN WE WERE GROWING UP IN WEST TEXAS, if we saw Aunt Lillie on Christmas Day, her first greeting would be, "Christmas Gift!" Or, if she saw us the Day *Before* Christmas, she might say, "Christmas Eve Gift!" Aunt Lillie was the second of Daddy's three sisters, and she enjoyed teasing us – her nieces and nephews -- when we were together at Christmas.

Saying "Christmas Gift!" was a carryover from Aunt Lillie's own childhood as she and my Daddy and their two other sisters were growing up in the first decade of the 20th century. The idea was this: On Christmas Day, if I saw you before you saw me and I called out, "Christmas Gift!" you were supposed to give me a present in addition to whatever you had already planned to give me.

After a while, the idea grew to include the Day *Before* Christmas. So, I was supposed to give you a present in advance if you saw me first and said, "Christmas Eve Gift!" Kids in that generation tried to get the jump on each other by calling out those expressions in hopes of gaining an extra present or two.

I didn't know whether this might have been strictly a local practice where Daddy and his sisters had grown up in northeastern Texas. But then, on the Internet, I came across references to this practice in the transcript of a tale told by the late John Henry Faulk, nationally famous Texas storyteller on National Public Radio.*

Faulk's story was about a poor white family who were given food from a charitable source at Christmastime. They shared their bounty with an African-American family down the road who had even less. A twelve-year-old boy said that, in addition to the meat and vegetables and desserts, "there was an apple and an orange and some stripety candy at everybody's place."

When the black family arrived, the father in the host family greeted his neighbor with, "Christmas Gift." Then, while the meal was being prepared, the children of both races played Christmas Gift as they ran around and around the house and rolled in the dirt.

The history of this tradition is somewhat murky, but many slave owners are reported to have encouraged their slaves to come to the "big house" and shout out "Christmas Gift" in expectation of receiving coins or other small gifts. George Washington is said to have used this little game as a way to give coins to his servants and slaves. There are also reports that British and Scottish immigrants brought the practice from their mother countries.

Ireland also can lay claim to the tradition. A woman recalled that her family came from "the Ould Sod" in 1839 when Texas was a republic. She said her mother continued the Christmas Eve Gift custom inherited from their Irish forebears. "My Irish mother hit the floor on Christmas Eve singing out 'Christmas

Eve Gift' to my Dad and me!" They expected to hear this, first thing, when sleepy eyes were just opening and they could never win the contest.

One woman who grew up on a farm said her dad was known to hide behind the smoke house and leap out at his grandchildren as they arrived on Christmas morning in order to say "Christmas Gift" first.

Another woman's family would yell, "Christmas Gift," when they visited other family homes instead of saying, "Hello."

In further checking the Internet, I learned this tradition is still alive and well in areas beyond Texas, across the Southwest and the South and even into the Midwestern states. One woman even played the game while living in Saudi Arabia.

Some families go at the game with a vengeance:

One woman told how her mom used to sneak up early in the morning and say, "Christmas Gift" before the daughter was really awake. Years later, her mother would call long-distance with the opening greeting, "Christmas Eve Gift," with a "gotcha" tone to her voice. The woman said her mother has been dead many years, but she still longs to hear that greeting on Christmas Eve.

Often, there is the serious expectation that the person who has been "got" is supposed to give some kind of gift.

A man in Texas said the gift doesn't have to be anything of value, but people are supposed to come up with a gift. One of his daughters loves to be on the gift-giving end, so she prepares little inexpensive gifts. Because she likes this so much, she coaxes someone in the family to say 'Christmas Eve Gift," so she can give the gift she has carefully wrapped. The father said it is fun just to act "dumb" and see how far his daughter will go in order to get you to say the magic words.　　Another man said of his great aunt, "Until the day she died at 94, she would answer every phone call on Christmas Eve with 'Christmas Eve Gift.' It's still a big deal to call my mother and her sister early in the morning on the 24th."

In Louisiana, a mother said her children set their alarms so they can get up early on Christmas Eve to try to be the one to get something to play with all day in anticipation of the big day tomorrow.

A kind of contest or battle developed between a mother and her college-age son. The mother said it's getting harder to get the best of him. "He has all the gadgets, such as caller ID and now knows when to answer "Christmas Eve Gift" before he says hello." So she started staying up late on the 23rd in order to email him a "Christmas Eve Gift" message at 12:01 a.m. on Christmas Eve.

Sometimes it takes a while for some who marry into the custom to warm up to the routine, but all this can create great family fun and anticipation year by year.

Perhaps we can find a serious Christian reflection based on this premise. In the Advent and Christmas season, we have opportunity to think of gifts God has given us across the years of our lives, not just "Christmas Eve Gifts" but gifts every day we've lived.

If we were to say "Christmas Eve Gift" to people in the first Christmas, what gifts would they have for us?

Mary's response could be the gift of faith which overcomes our fears.

Mary was perplexed when the angel Gabriel called her "favored one" and said, "God is with you." So his next words were, "Don't be afraid, Mary, for you have found favor with God." But she did not immediately lose her fear when he went on to say she was going to have a baby, the Son of the Most High.

She had heard other people -- mostly old people -- talk about holy visions or dreams. That was for folks who lived close to God. But now it happened to her. Imagine her thoughts: "Having a baby who has no human father? Who ever heard of that?" But then, she thought of Joseph. "How's he going to take this news? How can I make him believe this is true? He'll divorce me. He can have me stoned to death for being with another man, when I haven't *been* with another man in that way." Perhaps she lost sleep after the angel went away as questions kept running through her mind. But in time, she found the peace of God which passes understanding and faced this difficult future with faith.

If we were to say "Christmas Eve Gift" to Joseph, he could offer patience. He gained this gift after Mary shared her story with him. He knew the child she was carrying was not his, and he knew his legal right to expose her before the town officials. Instead, he claimed her as his wife after he, too, was visited by an angel who confirmed Mary's explanation.

Joseph can also offer us the more astounding "Christmas Eve Gift" of adoption.

On that first Christmas, Joseph gave Jesus the gift of sonship. After the birth stories, Joseph largely fades into the background. But he gave his own name to Jesus. The Gospels call Jesus the carpenter's son (Matthew 13:55; Mark 6:3) and the son of Joseph (Luke 3:23; John 1:45; 6:42).

Joseph wraps the strength of his character and his love

around all his children, including this son who comes to be called Emmanuel, God with us.

Jesus told stories which point to God as Loving Father who provides for the needs of his children. In the Sermon on the Mount (Matthew 7:9-11), Jesus draws this comparison:

Or what man of you, if his son asks him for bread, will give him a stone? Or if he asks for a fish, will give him a serpent? If you then, who are evil, know how to give good gifts to your children, how much more will your Father who is in heaven give good things to those who ask him!

Jesus pointed to God as the Father who forgives his children of their wrongdoings and welcomes them home when they stray. In stories such as the Prodigal Son (Luke 15), it seems unlikely Jesus would have used the father image as a picture of God unless He Himself in His own formative years had known a loving, caring, forgiving father.

Now consider this: Each one of us is an adopted child of God. It might seem that God is taking a risk in bringing you or me into His family. But God is the Loving Father beyond all loving fathers. And Joseph is our role model for trusting God's love. Jesus is the true Son of God. As His adopted brothers and sisters, we share the Father's love. An amazing "Christmas Gift!"

John Henry Faulk's Christmas Story: NPR. www.npr.org › Arts & Life › Holidays 2010 › NPR's Holiday Favorites

Reports on the "Christmas Eve Gift" tradition are available widely on the Internet including the following:

Christmas Eve Gift in other families
freepages.genealogy.rootsweb.ancestry.com/.../drawer-**christmaseve**..

Christmas Eve Gift www.gunblast.com/ChristmasEveGift.htm -

Christmas Eve Gift | The Midnight Cafe   www.themidnightcafe.
org/?p=1131

Christmas Eve Gift! | MetaFilter **www.metafilter.com/98894/Christmas-Eve-Gift**

The Other Wise Man

THE BIBLE STORY OF THE BIRTH OF JESUS is full of colorful characters and dramatic events: angels appearing to Mary, to Joseph, and to shepherds; the journey from Nazareth to Bethlehem; exotic star gazers from faraway lands; Herod's efforts to kill all the baby boys; the Holy Family's escape to Egypt.

All these elements have caught the imagination of singers and storytellers who construct fanciful narratives which go far beyond the biblical account. The resulting tales take on lives of their own which sometimes impact our understanding of what the Bible actually says.

A case in point: the Three Kings show up in carols and pageants, as well as in crechés near the Christmas tree. The Bible refers to Wise Men or Magi who come seeking the Baby who is born King of the Jews. They are astronomers or astrologers whose studies of the stars have led them from the east toward Bethlehem. But nowhere are these men identified as kings, and the only reference to the number three is the mention of three gifts they brought: gold, frankincense, and myrrh.

Still, this tradition of Three Kings prevails. The trio have been given names: Melchior, Casper, and Balthazar. The three are also identified as coming from different nations and races, as an indication that the birth of Jesus was for all humanity. This all-inclusiveness is a noble concept with a biblical basis, but we read between the lines when we mark the Kings/Magi as representatives of a variety of nationalities.

Poet and storyteller Henry Van Dyke expanded the number of star-followers from the traditional three to four. He wrote the fictional piece, "The Story of the Other Wise Man." Artaban, Van Dyke's "other," also sees the Star and agrees to rendezvous with the better-known fictional trio.

A Persian of great wealth and property, Artaban studied the skies and also practiced the healing arts. He sought to enlist other devout men of means to join him on his journey. He called his wealthy friends together to inform them of his plan to meet Melchior, Casper, and Balthazar and go in search of one who had been born King of the Jews. Artaban told his comrades of seeing a great light, the star he was convinced would lead them to this newborn King. He was to meet the others ten days hence, at a designated spot, no later than midnight on the tenth day. If anyone did not arrive by then, they all agreed the others should leave without him.

As a mark of his confidence and commitment to the quest, Artaban showed his peers three costly precious stones – a sapphire, a ruby, and a pearl – which he would give the infant King. He had sold all his goods and lands in order to follow his light to the wonder child.

To a man, his friends declined to join him in this search for a new King of the Jews. They called Artaban dreamer – and worse – belittling the idea that God would send such a King to an inconsequential land such as Judah. So, one by one, they left Artaban to his lonely quest.

This Other Wise Man's aging father said he was too old and frail to make the long and arduous journey. But he did not discourage his son. Referring to Artaban's light, the father warned that this might be "only a shadow of the light," as one of friends had said. The pilgrimage could end as an empty search.

Still, the father said, "it is better to follow even the shadow of the best than to remain content with the worst. And those who would see wonderful things must often be ready to travel alone."

As his friends were leaving, Artaban saw a radiant point of light in the sky, tiny and remote. But he was certain this was the star which would lead him to his King.

Artaban set out on his journey, realizing he needed the entire ten days if he hoped to connect with the other three at the designated time and place. Day after day, he pushed his favorite horse as hard as the animal could bear.

On the tenth night, about three hours before midnight, the horse slackened her pace as they came to a grove of date palms outside a city. She needed rest, but she also sensed something -- someone -- in need of help. They stopped, and Artaban dismounted, discovering a Jewish man in peasant's garb who was running a dangerously high fever.

At first, he was torn between pressing on to keep his appointment with the other magi or giving a cup of cold water to this poor, perishing man. But Artaban soon realized he had to use his medical skills if the man were to live. He worked hour after hour, so it was well past midnight before he was able to bring the man safely through this crisis. When the stranger was adequately revived, Artaban gave the man supplies of food and herbs and told him to go into the city and get further help.

With this delay, it was nearly sunup when the Other Wise Man arrived at the rendezvous point. To his dismay, Artaban found a note from his three friends. True to the plan the four had agreed on, they had left without him when the midnight hour passed.

Their meeting place was on the edge of a desert, so Artaban realized he could not survive if he tried to travel it alone. So he returned to the city, sold one of his valuable stones, the sapphire, and bought camels and provisions for the journey. Even as he made these preparations, he realized he might never find his friends, and -- more significantly -- he wondered whether he would ever find his King.

Still Artaban followed his star to Bethlehem. He found his way to the house where Mary, Joseph, and the Baby King had stayed. But he learned the other three men had come and gone, and the parents had fled to Egypt. King Herod was threatening to kill the boy babies because he feared the newborn King of the Jews would seek to take over his throne in Jerusalem.

In Bethlehem, Artaban found a young mother and child. He wondered whether this boy, rather than the child who had been taken to Egypt, might be his King. But these thoughts were interrupted when he heard loud noises of horses and riders on the street outside this humble residence. The mother was in panic as she realized these men were carrying out Herod's

An Angel Spoke

Lawrence Webb, 1934 -

Henry T. Smart, 1813-1879

1. An an - gel spoke to Ma - ry, "All Hail, Blest Vir - gin dear,
2. An an - gel spoke to Jo - seph, When he was lost in grief.
3. An an - gel spoke to shep - herds, A - mong their flock that night.
4. An an - gel speaks in our day: "To you a Child is born,

You soon will have a ba - by." His words brought her great fear.
The words were full of com - fort, They brought him deep re - lief.
The men came to the sta - ble, Awe - strick - en by the sight.
Go share the bless - ed tid - ings With those who are for - lorn:

"How can this be?" she asked him. "I've ne - ver been with man."
He jour - neyed far with Ma - ry And came to Beth - 'lem's town.
They knelt be - fore the Ba - by, As pa - rents hov - ered near.
This Child has come to save you, Down from His home a - bove.

The an - gel re - as - sured her, "All this is in God's plan."
There, in a low - ly man - ger, They laid their Ba - by down.
Then on their way, re - turn - ing, The shep - herds spread good cheer.
As you ac - cept His bless - ings, Your hearts will fill with love."

To Us a Child is Born

Lawrence Webb, 1934 -

Traditional Spanish Melody

1. To us a child is born, Al - le - lu - ia, A - men.
2. An - gels pro - claim the birth, Al - le - lu - ia, A - men.
3. Wise men come from a - far, Al - le - lu - ia, A - men.
4. Des - tined to bear a cross, Al - le - lu - ia, A - men.
5. Men, wo - men, ev' - ry - where, Al - le - lu - ia, A - men.

On this blest Christ - mas morn, Al - le - lu - ia, A - men.
Glad tid - ings for the earth, Al - le - lu - ia, A - men.
Fol - low - ing Beth - le'm's star, Al - le - lu - ia, A - men.
Sav - ing our souls from loss, Al - le - lu - ia, A - men.
Cast off your cold des - pair, Al - le - lu - ia, A - men.

He is the Prince of Peace, His coun - sel brings re - lease,
Spread good news of great joy, God's praise your tongues em - ploy,
Gold, in - cense, myrrh they bring, Gifts for the New - born King,
Through Christ, we're born a - gain, For - giv'n from ev' - ry sin.
Great joy for us to - day: His reign on earth holds sway,

His reign will nev - er cease, Al - le - lu - ia, A - men!
Go, wor - ship Ma - ry's boy, Al - le - lu - ia, A - men!
With them, we glad - ly sing, "Al - le - lu - ia, A - men!"
In Him we all are kin, Al - le - lu - ia, A - men!
New birth that makes us say, "Al - le - lu - ia, A - men!"

Lyrics ©2010 Lawrence Webb

orders and were coming to search out her baby next.

Artaban stood in the doorway as the soldiers came near. When they asked whether there was a baby in the house, Artaban assured them there was not. Then, to persuade them to be on their way, he gave their leader the ruby, the second stone he had purchased for the King.

This Other Wise Man felt doubly guilty: for lying to save the child's life and for giving up another stone he had intended for his Baby King. But he felt he had to do what he did.

With one stone remaining, Artaban went to Egypt, hoping to find the family who had fled from Bethlehem. His search went on for years, finding Jews in various countries who had been forced to leave their native land. Perhaps the King and his family were among their fellow displaced persons.

This Other Wise Man moved among the poor and needy, feeding the hungry, clothing the naked, healing the sick, and comforting the captives.

With the passing of the decades, as his travels continued, he often had visited Jerusalem, hoping the King might be there. Some thirty-three years after he had left his home, he was in Jerusalem yet again, at the Passover season.

Excitement was in the streets. He heard of three men who were going to be crucified outside the city wall. Two were common thieves. The third was a man called Jesus of Nazareth, who was condemned for insurrection because he claimed to be King of the Jews. Artaban pondered whether this man could be the King he had sought all these years. If so, the pearl might save the man from execution.

While these thoughts raced through his mind, human need once again crossed his path.

Amid the jostling throng on the way to Golgotha's hill, a young woman was fleeing her captors. She was being sold into slavery because her father had left a great debt when he died.

As they neared the site of the crucifixion, the woman threw herself at Artaban's feet. She said she recognized from his garb that he was a Magi because her father had also been a Magi.

For a third time, the Other Wise Man faced the choice of ministering to a desperate fellow human being or holding out in the hope of giving this last precious stone to his long-sought King.

Even as Artaban gave the woman the pearl to secure her freedom, Jerusalem was convulsed in an earthquake. A heavy tile, shaken loose from a roof, struck him on the temple. He crumpled to the ground, and the freed slave knelt beside him.

A distant voice, like music, came through the air, and the woman noticed the old man's lips moving as if in response to the heavenly sound. She heard Artaban saying these words:

Lord, when saw we thee an hungred, and fed thee? or thirsty, and gave thee drink? When saw we thee a stranger, and took thee in? or naked, and clothed thee? Or when saw we thee sick, or in prison, and came unto thee?

As the Other Wise Man was breathing his last, the young woman thought she heard these words in the air:

"Verily I say unto you, inasmuch as ye have done it unto one of the least of these my brethren, ye have done it unto me."

Although the figure of the Other Wise Man is built on Van Dyke's lively imagination, the story contains a firm biblical principle:

If you want to honor Jesus, find a needy person and help meet those needs.

That's what Henry Van Dyke tells us in his story.

That's what Jesus tells us in the words Van Dyke quotes from Matthew 25:37-40 as Artaban is dying.

Someone said Van Dyke combined the Christmas story with the story of the Good Samaritan to bring us "The Story of the Other Wise Man."

We may not have the sapphires, rubies, and pearls the Other Wise Man intended to give his King of the Jews. But we have our own good gifts of love and resources we can share to brighten someone's life at Christmas and all through the year.

The text of Henry Van Dyke's "The Story of the Other Wise Man" can be found at various sites online, including *Project Gutenberg*, http://www.gutenberg.org/catalog/world/readfile?fk_files=1477582

The Toy at the Bottom of the Stocking

CHARLOTTE DIAMOND IS A CANADIAN MUSICIAN and composer who shows great sensitivity for young children. [1]

In my perennial search for Christmas CDs, I found *The Christmas Gift*, a collection of fifteen of her songs of the season, at a garage sale. [2] The CD is appropriately named because it is a Christmas gift to anyone who loves Christmas, especially anyone who loves Christmas with children.

Ms. Diamond is a Pied Piper for children. With her trilingual speaking and singing, she lures children in French, Spanish, and English. The CD has sacred carols in all three of her languages, plus one in Zulu and "Silent Night" in its original German as well as English.

She is also a veritable children's ambassador to the United Nations, with all these nations represented on the CD, along with Peru and the Huron or Wyandot tribe from her native Canada. There are also secular songs of Christmas, and a song about a dreydl for Hanukkah.

With a lifelong interest in music, Ms. Diamond did folk music and was the opening act for singers such as Pete Seeger. Then, when her children came along, she began to write music for them. Then she went public with her original music. She has become well-known for her songs for children ages two through ten.

Her album titles offer play on words: *10 Carrot Diamond* and *Diamond in the Rough*. The song, "Four Hugs a Day," says "nobody gets enough hugs," and everyone needs at least four. That's the minimum, not the maximum. She developed her own record label with the hug tie-in: Hug Bug Records.

Other message songs, which resonate with parents who attend her concerts and buy her records, include "Leave the World a Little Better."

Ms. Diamond's Christmas composition which especially attracted my attention on *The Christmas Gift* CD is "The Toy at the Bottom of the Stocking," spoken rather than sung.

This story is consistent with the sensitivity expressed in the songs mentioned earlier. The narrator recalls children who hang stockings on Christmas Eve, then rush downstairs on Christmas morning to see what is in them.

They would find oranges at the top of the stockings, but there always were carefully wrapped small toys at the bottom. There might be other, bigger, toys too big to put in the stocking, but the toy at the bottom of the stocking was always the best.

Once, the toy at the bottom was a train which had belonged to Grandpa. Another time, it was a little bear. Yet again, a tiny picture book. Still another year, a collar for a new puppy.

As Ms. Diamond looked back on childhood Christmases, she realized that whatever the tiny toy might be at the bottom of the stocking, every year there was something even better: Love at the bottom of the stocking.

Gift-giving can readily get out of hand: Children come to expect more and more each year, and they lose sight of the true meaning of Christmas as the birth of Jesus. The dominant figure in the season is Santa Claus. If Jesus enters the picture at all, it is often with token mention. Someone has suggested that, with this emphasis on getting, the day might appropriately be called Giftmas. The Santa Claus buildup starts months in advance of December 25, with glittering packages placed under the tree days before the Big Event.

The day is probably gone forever when most children could be satisfied with small presents such as those Ms. Diamond writes about as "The Toy at the Bottom of the Stocking."

Certainly, there are countless numbers of homes in which children have to remain content with small, inexpensive gifts under their trees. In many other homes, parents should exercise restraint and select gifts more like the toy in the stocking. Instead, many parents buy presents they cannot afford and go into the new year with debts they have difficulty paying.

If love at the bottom of stacks of presents creates debt, the love is misdirected. If love at the bottom of stacks of presents leads children and youth to feel they deserve all this and more, that love, too, is unwisely expressed.

Such foolish expression of love may spring from the "Everybody's Doing It" syndrome, the need to "Keep Up with the Joneses." If we can afford expensive presents, or if we can juggle our credit cards until after January 1, we think, "Bigger is Better," as we buy presents to please our children and impress our neighbors and our children's friends.

In the aftermath of the holiday, we are asked, "Did you have a good Christmas?" All too often, we answer in terms of what we got, with no mention of spiritual benefits.

As long as the money is there or the checks don't bounce, this pattern likely will continue, as we sigh about "what we did for love." In reality, we rarely think of love as we open expensive presents. If there is love at the bottom of the stocking, it often is well-hidden.

Instead of Ms. Diamond's minimum four hugs a day, much of our hugging may come as we hug our loot to ourselves while the pile of wrapping paper mounts.

There is probably no realistic hope of changing the rampant commercial aspect of Christmas, short of a major national economic collapse leaving most of us without money.

Getting back to small presents and finding love at the bottom of the stocking will have to happen in individual families. Parents will have to find the courage to say "No" to excessive spending. This will not come easily – if it comes at all.

Any attempt to move away from the love of presents to the love of family and love of Jesus should not be done cold-turkey or by decree from the parents. A unilateral decision by the adults would bring about feelings remote from love.

If we hope to bring about such changes, this should be discussed by all members of the family months before the shopping season begins and before expectations have been building regarding hoped-for major presents.

Realistic scaling back might need to be phased in, rather than moving in one year from several elaborate gifts per person to one inexpensive or moderately priced gift for each family member.

As an alternative to excessive spending on each other, the family together might examine how much was spent the previous year and consider using a portion of that amount to benefit the homeless or a local charity. In place of several gifts per person, some families have put envelopes on the tree addressed to each person as a substitute for at least one gift. Inside the envelopes were names of local ministries to which a donation had been made in that family member's name.

In some cultures, gift-giving is kept separate from the celebration of the birth of Jesus. In Germany, Hungary, and the Netherlands, gifts are given by St. Nicholas on his day, December 6, almost three weeks before Christmas. In other countries, particularly Hispanic cultures, gifts are given by the Three Kings on January 6, the last of the Twelve Days of Christmas. This is traditionally the day the Kings or Wise Men arrived to give their gifts to the Baby King.

There might still be the temptation to overspend, regardless of the change of dates. But by moving gifts away from December 25, there would at least be the potential for making the familiar holiday more of a holy day.

If a family should decide to take some of these steps, they might more readily rediscover Ms. Diamond's Love at the Bottom of the Stocking, however simple or elaborate the tangible gifts.

> *In this the love of God was made manifest among us, that God sent his only Son into the world, so that we might live through him. In this is love, not that we loved God but that he loved us and sent his Son to be the expiation* [sacrifice] *for our sins* (1 John 4:9-10).

Thanks be to God for his inexpressible gift! (2 Corinthians 9:15).

---

[1] Charlotte Diamond's biographical information came from www.charlottediamond.com/catalog/printbio.html.

[2] Charlotte Diamond CD, *The Christmas Gift*, was produced by Charlotte Diamond Music Inc., 1990 CAPAC.

A Dismal Christmas Revisited

(Author's note: This story first appeared in my book, Christmas Memories from Seven to Seventy, *in 2008. See the copyright page for where to purchase the book. The story is reprinted here with some afterthoughts.)*

It was Christmas 1947. I was 13. I heard Daddy tell Mother that he was going to Sweetwater with Uncle Jim. When I asked if I could go, Daddy said, "No," with no explanation.

I said, "But I was hoping – "

Daddy again said, "No!"

With Daddy, "No" meant "No." I'd be in trouble if I said anything else about it.

It was Christmas Eve morning, and I hoped, if I went with him, I could get some money to buy presents.

Daddy put on his coat. Stepping out the door, he put on his hat and then lit a Camel cigarette before striking out up the road to Uncle Jim and Aunt Chessie's.

We were living in a rent house about a quarter of a mile

from their house. This was about the fifth boll pulling season that we had come to harvest their cotton crop.

I hated pulling cotton. I would much rather be in school.

As boll pulling came to an end each year, Daddy would start looking for a farm job. This year, he had made several visits with farmers around Sweetwater and Roscoe but hadn't come up with anything. So we were mainly sitting and waiting to see where we would finish out the school year.

I watched as Uncle Jim and Daddy drove by, feeling sorry for myself that I wasn't going along.

Lois Marie and Leonard Morris spent the day with our cousins up the road, and Lee Roy was off in the pasture hunting. So Mother and I were the only ones in the house. She was unusually quiet all through a long afternoon. I wondered why she wasn't listening to "Stella Dallas" and her other soap operas on the radio.

About four o'clock, Uncle Jim's car pulled into our yard. I expected Daddy to jump out and tell us to help him get the groceries into the house. Instead, Uncle Jim got out of his car and came toward our front door. Daddy wasn't with him.

Mother had been looking out the bedroom window, so she hurried outside and closed the door. She and Uncle Jim stood in the yard and talked quietly, then he got back in the car and she walked slowly back toward the house.

"Where's Daddy?"

Mother didn't answer. She brushed the hem of her apron across her face.

"What did Uncle Jim say?"

She still didn't answer as she hurried past me into their bedroom.

At supper, Mother was tight-lipped as we all asked about Daddy.

"Did Uncle Jim run off and leave him in town?" Lee Roy asked.

"When will Daddy be back?" Leonard Morris wanted to know.

Marie asked, "Is he okay?"

Mother looked pale and frightened as we finished the meal in silence.

I wanted to ask, "Is he ever coming back?" But I kept that question to myself.

As dark settled in, I saw the lights of a car coming down the road. Uncle Jim and Aunt Chessie and Mother stood out in the yard and talked a long time. They went back toward their house as

Mother came back inside.

She said little, but she started packing night clothes for all of us into a battered suitcase.

"What are you doing?"

"Where's Daddy?"

"Uncle Jim's car is out front!"

"Will we find Daddy?"

"We can't go off without Daddy, can we?"

We piled into the car with Uncle Jim, our questions still unanswered. Mother and Lee Roy sat in front with Uncle Jim.

At 13, I didn't like having to sit in the back with Lois Marie and Leonard Morris. They started singing "Jingle Bells" and "Santa Claus Is Coming to Town," so I couldn't hear what was being said up front about where we were going.

We drove through Roscoe and on to Sweetwater, the county seat.

"Are we gonna pick Daddy up in Sweetwater?"

"How will we know where he's at?"

When we reached Sweetwater, we didn't stop. As we headed south of town, we knew the answer:

"We're going to Grandma's!"

Then more questions:

"Is Daddy out there with her?"

"Why didn't he wait for us?"

By the time we got to Grandma's farm out on the Divide, about eighteen miles south of town, it seemed like the middle of the night.

"There's no light on."

"You think Grandma's gone somewhere, too?"

As we pulled into her yard, I thought I saw a dim light inside her house.

Mother hurried to the door. She rattled the screen door and called out, "Momma! Momma!"

Grandma was holding a coal oil lamp as she opened the door and said, "Forever and forever! I never expected to see you all on Christmas Eve. The Lord have mercy!"

She led the way through the side room into the center room of the little three-room house. She set the lamp down on the dresser. After speaking briefly with Uncle Jim, she started making places
for us to sleep.

Mother said, "Jim, all I can say is, 'Thanks until you're better paid.'"

"That's all right, Vandelia," Uncle Jim said. "That's all right. You shouldn't have to spend Christmas by yourselves that way."

It felt like home at Grandma's. In between Daddy's farm jobs, we often came back here to live with Mother's mother. So, just being here took away much of the gloom after Daddy didn't come

home.

Next morning, Grandma handed out candy and nuts and gave each of us a dollar bill. That was all our presents, since Daddy hadn't come home.

Grandma had a neighbor, Judson Modrall, working her place "on the halves," but she had a cow and some chickens, and she canned things from her garden. So she had plenty on hand to make a big Christmas dinner at noon.

Not long after we ate, Lee Roy looked out the window and said, "There's Uncle Jim's car."

I ran to the window. Almost before Uncle Jim stopped, Daddy jumped out and started toward the

house, almost in a run. He was red in the face as he burst into the big room and yelled at Mother, "What in the devil did you mean, leaving home like that?"

Lee Roy said to me, under his breath, "What in the devil did *you* mean, leaving home like that?

I whispered back, "Better not let him hear you say that."

"Let's go home," Daddy said.

Grandma asked, "Travis, would you and Jim like some chicken and dressing before you all go?"

Daddy frowned and didn't answer. I could tell he didn't want to stay, but Uncle Jim said, "That would be real nice, Mrs.

Roberts. Thank you."

Mother and Grandma pulled our things together while the men folks ate. By the time we got in the car, Daddy had cooled down some.

As we rode home, Leonard Morris and Lois Marie started singing again, drowning out the possibility of my asking the question we were afraid to ask: Why had Daddy gone off on Christmas Eve?

* * *

This true story has consistently drawn more comments than any other story in that earlier book. Many people have asked: "Where *did* your Daddy go? Why didn't he come home that Christmas Eve?"

My consistent answer has been, "I don't know. I've told you everything I know about it. You didn't ask Daddy questions. Mother may have known, but I never asked her."

Like many of the stories in that Christmas memories book and this present book, "A Dismal Christmas" was first read by a Sunday afternoon writers group which meets at Anderson University, where I was a professor for twenty-three years. We distribute copies of our materials to the group and read our writing out loud as others follow along.

When I finished reading the "Dismal" story to the critiquing group, Lu Oliver, a faithful member, cried out: "It can't end like that, Larry. You've got to have a happy ending."

"Lu," I replied, " that's what happened. That's the way it ended. I wasn't happy with the ending. But this is a true experience, not a 'lived-happily-ever-after' story."

Many of us have prayed the prayer from Psalm 90 with

reference to our Christmas celebrations: *Make us glad as many days as thou hast afflicted us, and as many years as we have seen evil. Let thy work be manifest to thy servants, and thy glorious power to their children* (Psalm 90:17-18).

As much as we would like to think otherwise, we have no guarantee that the scales of justice will balance and that God, in the prayer of that psalm, will *"Make us glad as many days as you have afflicted us."*

I hope both my friend Lu and you as you read this book have more pleasant Christmas memories than unhappy ones to look back on. This Christmas, you may be in a house overflowing with multigenerational relatives. Or you may be with family and friends only in memory as you are separated by miles or by death.

Whether you feel the presence or by the absence of those you hold dear, I hope you can call to mind the Baby born that first Christmas who was called Emmanuel, which means "God with us." May the light of His presence brighten every Christmas for you.

Have Yourself a *Blessed* Little Christmas

THIS IS A STORY IN FOUR SCENES, in which a pessimistic secular Christmas song morphed into a positive affirmation of faith in Jesus Christ.

"Have Yourself a Merry Little Christmas" has three distinctly different versions as well as one with only minor changes from the most famous version.

Scene One: Hugh Martin, with impressive credentials as a writer of musicals for Broadway and for Hollywood, wrote the original version of this song and other music for the 1944 movie, *Meet Me in St. Louis.* [1]

Scene Two: Judy Garland was supposed to sing "Have Yourself a Merry Little Christmas" in the film. However, when she saw the words, she asked the composer to make some changes. After some hesitation, Mr. Martin gave in.

Scene Three: Some years later, when Frank Sinatra was planning to record the song, he asked for more changes: A small number of words, but significant for the content.

Scene Four: Martin made the final major change many

years later at his own initiative. This rewrite dramatically altered the theme of the song as it reflected a major change in Martin's outlook on life.

In the movie, as Christmas approaches, a family is upset when the authoritarian father springs the news that they are moving from St. Louis to New York City. With little regard for their feelings, he assures his wife and children: they will like their new home and have lots more money. But the move will mean breaking up friendships and courtships. One of the older sisters is hoping to get engaged almost any minute, so she doesn't know how that romance will be affected.

Against this background, Judy Garland sings the song to her on-screen younger sister, child star Margaret O'Brien, in the attempt to cheer her up about the impending move.

Trying to capture this dismal mood, Martin wrote some very dismal words in the original version. For example, they are urged to have "a merry little Christmas" because it may be their last. When they go to New York, they all may be "living in the past." Their faithful friends will be near to them "no more" instead of "once more," as it is sung in a later version.

The song offers the bottom line: The family will be together "if the Lord allows." Meantime, they will "have to muddle through somehow" in the effort to be merry.

No wonder Judy Garland didn't want to sing these thoroughly pessimistic lyrics in a wartime movie which was calculated to bring cheer to the country. Despite Garland's star power, Martin at first balked at her request. He said it took a while to get over his hurt pride at being edited – a sentiment any writer can identify with.

Then, after nursing his bruised ego for a while, Hugh

Martin obliged the film's name star and came up with the well-known words which are preserved on film and were the standard version of the song as recorded by many well-known artists.

There's still a melancholy undercurrent in this version, acknowledging Christmas this year isn't going to be what the family had hoped for. But a chin-up hope or wish is expressed twice: "next year," with light hearts and gaiety, troubles will be "far away" or "out of sight."

In this revised version, dependence on God is replaced with leaving the outcome to fate: "If the Lord allows" is changed to "if the fates allow." But the bottom line, in both the original and in the version that made it to the screen, is still that they'll be muddling through.

Sinatra recorded the movie version of the song in 1947 after it had found its way into popular usage. Then, a decade later, he was planning to include the song in an album called *A Jolly Christmas*, but he didn't think the lyrics were "jolly" enough. So he prevailed upon Martin to do some more editing and "jolly it up" for him. The main change this time was to remove the line about muddling and replace it with hanging a star on the tree in order to be merry. Also, the "Sinatra" version did away with the need to wait till "next year" when troubles would be gone. Instead of "next year," their troubles will disappear "from now on." These "jollier" words are more commonly used these days, but the fates rather than the Lord are still the determining factor in achieving the desired goal.

Though Martin had attained fame and wealth through his music, he was not content within himself as he moved in entertainment circles. He said this environment was "wonderful in a way but very temporal, very superficial . . . a very self-centered existence." [2]

This inability to reconcile himself to the kind of life he was living brought him to what he calls "a full-blown nervous breakdown" in 1960. With a feeling of utter helplessness in his own strength, he began praying to God for help. In working through this experience, he emerged with faith in Christ. A few years later, Martin became closely identified with Seventh Day Adventists.

With this reorientation of his life, Martin later wrote an entirely different version of his old song. In 2001, at the age of 86, using the same familiar tune, he wrote "Have Yourself a Blessed Little Christmas," with a forthright Christian message: [3] You should "Have yourself a blessed little Christmas" because Christ is born. So your voices should ring out on the happy morning.

This unapologetic Christian approach to Christmas refers to "hymns and hallelujahs" and "carols soaring up into the sky."

Now, instead of having a merry little Christmas "if the fates allow," the new song calls us to make music as "mighty as the heavens allow" in order to have that "blessed little Christmas." Each of these four versions of this song reflects an attitude some people have as they attempt "a merry little Christmas."

Original version: With life heavily bearing down, we may not be able to cope with Christmas. We associate the holiday with good cheer and light heartedness. When that balance is upset, the season may be too much to contend with, and this version reflects that discouragement. It may prove especially difficult to face the first Christmas after the death of someone dear. If a loved one died in the holiday season, every Christmas may be painful for family gatherings during holidays. Muddling may be the best we can do.

Movie version: Sometimes life seems to get put on hold, with loss of a job, an extended hospitalization, or a family member away in military service. In these situations, celebration of Christmas may be delayed until the absent loved one is able to be with the family or circle of special friends. For some, Christmas is specifically identified with a family gathering and exchange of presents. So they may say, "We had our Christmas a week early before Ralph had to go back to Afghanistan" or "We waited about Christmas till Shirley got out of the hospital." The family in the movie feels life being reduced to a freeze frame. A lot of muddling.

Sinatra's Version: The theme in this version seems to be, "Life is what you make it, so we're gonna hang that star on the treetop, come what may." There's no indication that this is the star of Bethlehem which guided the Wise Men. It may simply be the star on which we wish for a better day. This is akin to a later Christmas song, from Broadway's *Mame*: "We Need a Little Christmas." so it's time to "haul out the holly," "slice up the fruitcake," and put up the brightest lights they've ever seen in the attempt to find merriment when there seems to be little justification for merriment.[4]

Blessed Christmas Version: Here, the focus is on the real "original" version of Christmas. With so many superficial approaches to the season, the birth of Jesus can easily get buried. Hugh Martin's decision to use the familiar tune, with its secular connotations, as the basis for a positive Christian song is a dramatic testimony to the change in his life.

The lyrics of "Have Yourself a Blessed Little Christmas" point to Jesus as "Son of God/ And a friend to all," the heart of the Christmas message. There's no more hoping to get through the season "if the fates allow," no more muddling in order to have a merry Christmas.

Family gatherings with feasts and presents under the tree can be wonderful experiences in and of themselves, filled with rich fellowship and deep emotion. Infused with the awe and wonder of the Son of God coming into the world as a friend to all, those events can be more wonderful, enabling us to have truly "a blessed little Christmas."

Although there are no passages specifically indicated as songs in the Christmas stories in the Bible, many passages have been set to music. We imagine the angels sang "Glory to God in the Highest" when they brought "good news of great joy" which would be "for all people."

Also Mary's lengthy words of praise in Luke 1:46-55 are widely believed to be a song. It is traditionally known as "The Magnificat," based on the opening words, "My soul magnifies the Lord." Magnificat is the Latin word for magnify or make great.

Here are the opening verses: "*My soul magnifies the Lord, and my spirit rejoices in God my Savior, for he has regarded the low estate of his handmaiden. For behold, henceforth all generations will call me blessed; for he who is mighty has done great things for me, and holy is his name*" (vv. 46-49).

After the initial shock of learning of her impending motherhood, Mary's song indicates she will have herself "a blessed little Christmas."

---

[1] *Meet Me in St. Louis* (1944) - Trivia - IMDb www.imdb.com/title/tt0037059/trivia

[2] http://news.adventist.org/2005/12/culture-have-yourself-a-blesse-little-christmas-composer-hugh-marti-a-siger-el-elker-recollect.html

[3] http://www.answers.com/topic/have-yourself-a-merry-little-christmas#ixzz1Dkn0xhuh

[4] Jerry Herman, "We Need a Little Christmas," *Mame*. New York: Random House, 1966.

Not Your Usual Christmas Letter

THE TYPICAL FAMILY CHRISTMAS LETTER sounds as if the family hired a PR firm to write it: stressing all the wonderful things which have happened to all the wonderful members of our family this past year and how we look forward to even more wonderful things in the Happy New Year.

We expect – or at least think the readers of our Letter expect – a glowing report on the success and happiness all the family members have enjoyed since our last Letter.

On the other hand, Dave and Stephanie's annual epistle took a different turn when they learned Dave had a brain tumor. They didn't try to mask reality. They said, up front, "Life has played hardball with us this year."*

It probably was a shock to those who had not been in touch with the couple as they read:

"There were days we thought we would collapse from the pressure, the pain, and the fear. Somehow we found the strength and the courage to face each day. Some of those days were hopeful, and others were desperate."

They said they had "experienced every emotion to its extreme, except for loneliness." They were spared that because family and friends "ensured that we have never felt alone in our trials." Rather, these supporters had been "like a warm blanket on the coldest night."

Dave and Stephanie said they had a task to complete as they were to celebrate Christmas and New Year's: "It is time to put away past suffering, cherish what we have learned, and look forward with fresh hope." In the midst of all they had been through, they felt, "The season affords us that time—to close the door on the pain, yet always remember that we are stronger for having lived through it together."

Apparently, coming to terms with serious illness had taught them that "Christmas is so much more than the traditional exchanging of gifts.

"It is a time to step back and realize how very lucky we are to have life. Too often we take each other for granted, and forget that without each other, life has little meaning."

Their Christmas wish for their friends was "that you cherish those you love, and remember that the past has no power over us, the present is a gift, and the future holds hope and joy."

In view of Dave's illness they said, "The new year promises renewal of strength to fight our battle with cancer. We have learned that together we can achieve anything, and together we have nothing to fear, and together we have the power to overcome any challenge put before us."

Their closing words to their friends were these: "God has blessed our lives with people like you who have held us in our times of need, and laughed with us in our times of joy. We carry all of you with us in our hearts daily."

In spite of this cruel disease which was eating away at Dave's total physical being – or perhaps because of the cancer – this couple found strength they probably didn't know they had. If they had thought about such a possibility beforehand, they might have felt it would be more than they could bear.

They had the blanket-like warmth of family and friends, and, though their letter is not saturated with pious phrases, they found a deeper meaning, a sustaining grace, through their faith.

Facing Christmas with cancer could not have been easy, even with their faith in Christ.

Often, we come to Christmas, hoping to paper over the problems we are facing. We like to think, in the words of Hugh Martin's "Have Yourself a Merry Little Christmas," that "Next year all our troubles will be far away." (See an essay about that song on page 118.)

We invest the holiday season with much more freight than it is likely to be able to bear when we strive to make everything "merry and bright" the last week of the year.

In "O Little Town of Bethlehem," Phillips Brooks declared, "the hopes and fears of all the years are met in thee tonight." If we try to have those fears hermetically sealed off during the festive season, they will break loose and come back in January, like the charges on our credit cards, past due and with penalties accumulating.

We can learn from Dave and Stephanie's letter: Life does indeed play hardball with us at times. When we find ourselves in that game, we probably aren't ready to play.

This couple had loving friends and Christian parents to stand with them. But in that standing, these supporters were blown away just like the young cancer patient and his wife. Fortunately, these friends and family members offered no cold comfort of simplistic answers or false hope for the new year.

Instead, the couple said in their letter that they looked forward to the new year. Not that they would be home free, not that "next year all our troubles will be out of sight." Rather, they said that "the new year promises renewal of strength to fight our battle with cancer."

Again, as in Brooks's carol, the hopes and fears are both there. They've met on the dark streets of Bethlehem and on our dark streets as well. So it comes down to these questions: Which will gain the upper hand on our dark streets? Will we be battered down by fear, or will we see the everlasting light of hope shining from that stable?

St. Paul writes of faith and grace and hope in the fifth chapter of Romans:

> *Therefore, since we are justified by faith, we have peace with God through our Lord Jesus Christ. Through him we have obtained access to this grace in which we stand, and we rejoice in our hope of sharing the glory of God. More than that, we rejoice in our sufferings, knowing that suffering produces endurance, and endurance produces character, and character produces hope, and hope does not disappoint us, because God's love has been poured into our hearts through the Holy Spirit which has been given to us* (Romans 5:1-5).

It's no easy step to reach the point of saying with Paul, *we rejoice in our sufferings*. It's questionable whether Dave rejoiced in his cancer. But Paul made that statement after he had found grace to help in time of need. He said he could rejoice because he had discovered suffering can lead to endurance; endurance builds character; and hope is born out of this chain of experience.

Sometimes, people tend to equate hoping with wishing. They take exception to Tennyson's "Crossing the Bar," which says: "I *hope* to see my Pilot face to face/ When I have crossed the bar." These people also have problems with "Whispering Hope"with its admonition to "Hope for the sunshine tomorrow/ after the shower is gone." But if they study the Bible more carefully, they realize the last stanza of "Whispering Hope" is a paraphrase of Hebrews 6:19-20:

Which hope we have as an anchor of the soul, both sure and stedfast, and which entereth into that within the veil, Whither the forerunner is for us entered, even Jesus, made an high priest forever after the order of Melchisedec (KJV).

As the song suggests, hope often does come with a whisper, not with a shout. But it can burst into a shout as it takes root within us.

Surrounded by the love of family and friends, Dave and Stephanie came to realize: "Christmas is so much more than the traditional exchanging of gifts."

No doubt, one of the untraditional gifts they received through the warmth of human love was this gift of the hope which does not disappoint, as God's love was poured into their hearts through the gift of the Holy Spirit.

From R. Kirby Godsey, *When We Talk About God . . . Let's Be Honest.* Macon, Georgia: Smyth & Helwys Publishing, Inc., 1996, p. 100. Used with permission.

A Christmas Carol: A Christmas Parable

WE USUALLY LOOK AT THE EARLY CHAPTERS of Matthew and Luke for Christmas inspiration from Scripture. But there's an unsettling passage from Luke 12 we need to hear at Christmas:

> *And he said to them, "Take heed, and beware of all covetousness; for a man's life does not consist in the abundance of his possessions." And he told them a parable, saying, "The land of a rich man brought forth plentifully; and he thought to himself, `What shall I do, for I have nowhere to store my crops?' And he said, `I will do this: I will pull down my barns, and build larger ones; and there I will store all my grain and my goods. And I will say to my soul, Soul, you have ample goods laid up for many years; take your ease, eat, drink, be merry.' But God said to him, `Fool! This night your soul is required of you; and the things you have prepared, whose will they be?' So is he who lays up treasure for himself, and is not rich toward God."* (Luke 12:15-21).

This parable from Jesus may remind us of a notorious character from Charles Dickens. Ebenezer Scrooge, who haunts the scene at Christmas, is a businessman in London, not a country farmer. But the man in the biblical story and the central character in *A Christmas Carol* are blood brothers, if not exactly identical twins.

Dickens took the name *Scrooge* from a word which meant *crowding* or *squeezing*. The author describes Scrooge as "tight-fisted . . . a squeezing, wrenching, grasping, scraping, clutching, covetous, old sinner!" He is so cold-hearted that Dickens says, "He carried his own low temperature always about with him," in summer and winter.

Scrooge's internal coldness affects the physical environment of his office where he keeps only a small fire burning. His clerk Bob Cratchit sits in the back room, far away from Scrooge's little fire. On Christmas Eve, Cratchit bundles himself up as best he can, trying in vain to warm himself from the flame of a candle on his desk. The only way Cratchit could get to any coal for a fire would be to go by Scrooge's desk, and he knows Scrooge would object to his getting the coal.

Scrooge is so lacking in the spirit of "peace on earth, good will toward men" that he protests when his nephew Fred wishes him Merry Christmas. Scrooge tells Fred, Christmas is a humbug, and he wishes anyone who says, "Merry Christmas" should have "a stake of holly through his heart." When Cratchit asks for Christmas Day off, Scrooge grudgingly grants the request, complaining all the while.

Like the rich farmer, Scrooge thinks only of himself. When visitors come to his shop, asking help for the destitute, Scrooge asks them whether there are no prisons or workhouses where such people can be sent. "It's enough for a man to understand his own business, and not to interfere with other people's." And so he makes no pledge.

At the end of the work day on Christmas Eve, when Scrooge goes home to his cold, dark house, he is startled by a visit from the ghost of Jacob Marley, his seven-years-dead partner. Dickens says Marley was "dead as a door-nail." Marley had been as obsessed with money as Scrooge. The ghost is bound in a chain made of cash-boxes, keys, padlocks, ledgers, deeds, and purses made of steel.

The ghostly partner says of himself that, while he was alive, his spirit never ventured beyond their counting-house. He asks out loud why he walked on the street through crowds with his eyes turned down, never raising them to the star which led the Wise Men. He wonders whether the light of that star might have led him to homes where he could have helped needy families.

Scrooge's only hope for escaping a similar fate will be visits by ghosts from Christmases past, present, and yet to come, Marley tells him.

First comes the Ghost of Christmas Past who takes him out into the cold winter night. With this tour guide, Scrooge is reminded of his selfish deeds, such as refusing to give a young caroler something to brighten his Christmas.

When Scrooge sees his former employer, Fezziwig, giving Christmas bonuses, Scrooge regrets being so inconsiderate of his clerk, Bob Cratchit.

In another scene from the past, Ebenezer is with a young lady he might have married. She says his love for gold has replaced her in his heart. She had watched as his noble aspirations fell away and greed and gain replaced them.

The visit to the past causes Scrooge to see how his obsession with money engulfed him so that he has no time for romantic love or friendship. So he begins to face up to what his life has become.

Next, the Ghost of Christmas Present takes Scrooge to see the simple but joyous observance at Bob Cratchit's. The clerk has scraped together enough from the meagre salary from Scrooge to buy a Christmas goose. Cratchit's large family of children includes a frail little crippled boy called Tiny Tim. Dickens says Bob Cratchit looked "as if he loved the child, and wished to keep him by his side, and dreaded that he might be taken from him."

With the goose, the Cratchits have apple sauce, mashed potatoes, and a rich plum pudding. They end the meal as Bob Cratchit offers a toast to "Mr. Scrooge, the Founder of the Feast!" Mrs. Cratchit says she'd like to give Scrooge a piece of her mind to feast on. Then Tiny Tim asks a blessing: "God Bless Us, Everyone!"

Scrooge is moved by this toast, and he asks the Ghost whether Tiny Tim will live. The Ghost says he sees a vacant seat in the chimney-corner and "a crutch without an owner." Unless conditions change, the little boy will die.

The present-day vision also shows coal miners, who sing joyous carols, despite their poverty. At a lighthouse, two lonely watchmen likewise celebrate the true meaning of the season.

Scrooge also sees his nephew happily celebrating with his family. The nephew recounts how Uncle Scrooge called Christmas a "humbug." When other family members criticize Scrooge, Fred insists he has nothing to say against his uncle.

Moreover, the nephew wishes Uncle a Merry Christmas, even if Scrooge will not take it from him. Then all the family drink a toast to Uncle Scrooge.

In the final vision of the present, Scrooge sees a poverty-stricken boy and girl so thin and wrinkled, they almost seem to be elderly. When Scrooge asks, "Have they no refuge or resource?" the Spirit echoes the off-putting question Ebenezer had asked the men who sought donations for the poor: "Are there no prisons? . . . Are there no workhouses?" With that, the second Spirit vanishes.

With the Ghost of Christmas Yet To Come, Scrooge is led again to the Cratchit home. Fred, Scrooge's nephew is with the family, offering consolation. By following the conversation, Scrooge realizes Tiny Tim has died.

In another scene in this vision of the future, Scrooge overhears people talking unsympathetically about someone else who has died. One man calls the deceased "Old Scratch," a nickname for the devil. Then Scrooge is led to a rundown smelly, dirty area. He and the Spirit come to a shop where iron, old rags, bottles, bones and the like are bought.

Two women and a man enter the shop with goods they want to sell. The man has little more than a pencil case, a pair of sleeve buttons, and a brooch. One of the women has sheets and towels, some wearing apparel, two old-fashioned silver teaspoons, sugar tongs, and some boots. With the other woman, it becomes obvious that all three traders have come from a dead man's house where they took whatever they thought might be of value. This second woman had taken blankets and curtains which had surrounded the bed to provide privacy for the sleeper. But the woman took these bed clothes while the corpse was still in the bed. She even took the night shirt off the dead man.

If any doubt remains in Scrooge's mind as to the identity of the corpse, the spirit leads him to the window of his own office. When he looks in, he sees another man in his old chair. Then, to complete the picture, the spirit leads him to a gravestone with "Ebenezer Scrooge" engraved on it.

With this scene before him, Scrooge vows he will alter his life, honoring Christmas in his heart and keeping it all year long. As he pleads with this third Spirit, Scrooge wakes up to discover these three ghostly visitors all were simply in his dream. So he renews his vows to live differently.

And live differently, he does, beginning immediately: It is Christmas Day, so he orders a large turkey sent to the Cratchit home. Out on the street, he encounters the man who had sought the donation to charity the day before. He apologizes to the man and commits to a large contribution to help the needy.

In other signs of a changed heart, Scrooge goes to church, greeting people as he walks about the streets and patting children on their heads. Furthermore, he goes to his nephew's home and makes amends with Fred and his family. The next day at the office, Scrooge greets Bob Cratchit warmly, promises him a raise, and says he will assist Bob's family. He also orders Bob to kindle more fire and to keep enough coal to maintain the fires and keep the office warm. Unlike the bad dream, Tiny Tim did not die, and Scrooge becomes like a second father to the lad.

As we think of comparisons between Ebenezer Scrooge and

the rich farmer, we know each man cared for his own wealth and cared nothing for others.

The farmer congratulated himself for his wealth and looked to the future when he would *relax, eat, drink, be merry.* Though the old Scrooge was not the sort to make merry, he resembles the rich farmer in his obsession with holding on to his wealth for selfish purposes.

As we recall Scrooge's vision of his own death and the scavengers who pick over his few remaining possessions, we think of what God said to the rich farmer:

"You fool! This very night your life is being demanded of you. And the things you have prepared, whose will they be?" So it is with those who store up treasures for themselves but are not rich towards God.'

Dickens does not use the biblical term *repentance.*   But repentance is there because the biblical meaning involves a change of mind and a change of direction. After Scrooge is made to consider the whole sweep of his life -- past, present, and future -- his attitude toward his fellow humans undergoes a drastic change. His attitude regarding his possessions changes. He is no longer the "tight-fisted" person Dickens describes at the beginning. Instead, as we have seen, Scrooge is eager to help the less fortunate, including giving Bob Cratchit a decent living wage. He also contributes to charitable causes he previously rebuffed.

The central story in *A Christmas Carol* is a reflection of Charles Dickens's deep concern for the less fortunate. The author's care as an adult was influenced in no small way by hard times he endured as a child. At one point, his father was put in debtors' prison. The Cratchit house is thought to have been modeled after the small house in the London suburb of Camden Town where Dickens lived as a child. The Cratchit children also parallel the author's siblings, with Tiny Tim representing Charles's youngest, sickly brother, "Tiny Fred."*

The author's desire to improve the status of the poor shines through in *A Christmas Carol. This compassion* is also seen in his earlier novels, with the boys in the workhouse in *Oliver Twist* and with the deplorable conditions of children in schools in *Nicholas Nickleby.*

Dickens had a double motivation when he wrote *A Christmas Carol.* Because he was known for his concern for the plight of the poor, he had been asked to write an appeal for donations to charity. The final version of that appeal was the Scrooge story. He was also facing personal financial difficulty which provided additional motivation.

In this morality story, Ebenezer Scrooge is the embodiment of the selfish wealthy class who could not be bothered by the needs of those without resources. Likewise, Bob Cratchit's family stands for all who struggle from one pay period to the next.

The story has become an entertainment classic, but it also bears a central moral and spiritual lesson. Scrooge's physical and spiritual awakening on Christmas morning leads to a genuine compassion for the needy like that of the author.

Scrooge's promise of a raise in salary for Bob Cratchit comes on December 26, the day after Christmas, St. Stephen's Day, which the Brits observe as Boxing Day. This is a day people give boxes of food and other staples to those in need. Scrooge's action on that day seems to reflect that pattern of helping the less fortunate.

We readily respond to the call to provide food baskets at Thanksgiving and Christmas. But Scrooge's actions on Christmas Day and the day after indicate a continuing commitment beyond one or two special days of the year.

Christ said there is a special place in His kingdom for those who feed the hungry, clothe the naked, give water to the thirsty, welcome the stranger, and visit the sick and the prisoner. Scrooge had joined the fellowship of those who care for "the least of these" brothers and sisters of the Christ of Christmas (Matthew 25:37-40).

Dickens says of Scrooge's new way of life, "he knew how to keep Christmas well, if any man alive possessed the knowledge."

The author and his lead character set a worthy example for all who would "keep Christmas well." As we seek to follow that example, we will pray with Tiny Tim: "God Bless Us, Everyone!"

---

[1] "Facts behind **Dickens**' book, 'A Christmas Carol' " www.hollowhill.com › real haunted places › uk ghosts

[2] "The text of Charles Dickens's *A Christmas Carol* is available online at various sources, including http://www.gutenberg.org/ebooks/search/."

Someone Who'll Watch Over Me

"I'LL BE HOME FOR CHRISTMAS, If Only in My Dreams" would be an appropriate title for one of the scenes in a play about three political prisoners. The actual title, *Someone Who'll Watch Over Me*,[1] is almost identical with George and Ira Gershwin's love song popular in the 1950s, "Someone to Watch Over Me."[2]

Throughout the play, by Irishman Frank McGuinness, the men rely heavily on their memories, including Christmas memories. One reviewer said memory is a tool they use as they "struggle to maintain their sanity, humanity, and hope in a setting devoid of all three."[3]

The setting certainly suggests difficulty in preserving any of those human qualities. During the Lebanon hostage crisis in the 1980s, the men are taken prisoner without explanation, then brought, one by one, into a room somewhere in Beirut and chained to the wall.

Michael, the eldest, is from England, a university professor of Old English and its myths. Edward is an Irish journalist. Adam is an American physician. They did not know each other before their capture.

They hear their captors but never see them, and they are sure their captors hear them and keep track of all they do and say. This is one of the meanings of the play's title: They are sure someone is watching over them – with a less than benevolent intent.

All three men are from religious backgrounds, but their attitudes toward faith are different. Edward, with his Irish Catholic background, declares he hates all religion because it's bad for you. Michael finds meaning in his Anglican faith, but he is generally reticent regarding his personal life, including religion. Adam is most expressive about religious matters, though we are not told his specific orientation. He reads the Bible and the Koran, the only two books their captors let them have. When he sings "Amazing Grace," both Edward and Michael thank him.

Edward offers a kind of prayer for deliverance from those who believe in a God who is not merciful or compassionate (obviously his view of Islam). He prays further, "if they're wrong, God help them. And if they're right, God help us."

Both Adam and Edward bully Michael. Edward is especially hostile about the long history of England's persecution of Ireland. Both the younger men lace their vocabularies with obscenities and talk frankly about sex and their sexual desires. Michael asks them to stop swearing, complaining they have influenced him to start using such language. But then, he apologizes and refers to himself as sanctimonious.

Amid their differences, they learn to accommodate each other and rely on mutual memories and imaginations. They relive famous horse races and the 1977 Ladies' Final tennis match at Wimbledon. They enjoy an imaginary cocktail hour and write imaginary letters home.

In addition to Adam's hymns, the men sing "The Water is Wide," "For He's a Jolly Good Fellow," and "Run, Rabbit, Run." On this last song, Michael scurries around on the floor, as far as his chain permits, in the attempt to be a rabbit. Edward says he's more like a kangaroo.

Adam is taken away, and the other two wonder whether he was killed or given his freedom. They tend to think he is dead.

From the start of their internment, Michael has tried to keep track of the passing days, and when he says it is Christmas, Edward starts singing "Jingle Bells" and "O Come, All Ye Faithful."

Edward asks whether Michael is sure it is Christmas. When Michael assures him it is, Edward says their Muslim captors will probably leave them alone for the day, even though they don't celebrate Christmas.

As he thinks about the conflict between Christians and Muslims and about being held by Muslims, Edward is bitter. He says they wouldn't have been taken as prisoners if they had been Muslims. So he blames Jesus for this imprisonment; then he blames his own parents for raising him Catholic. Then he starts singing "O Come, All Ye Faithful" again.

This leads Edward to further expression of uncertainty. He quotes the angels' message of peace on earth; good will to all men. Then he vents more of his uncertainty about his incarceration and about Christmas. He asks Michael to tell him what peace is.

When Michael doesn't respond, Edward answers his own

question: Peace would be his if he were home with his wife at Christmas. He dreams of having sex with her and of their conceiving a child (in the words of the song) "on Christmas day in the morning."

Edward's thoughts then turn to smoking. Before his capture, he smoked forty cigarettes a day. Now, he has no access to cigarettes. He wonders whether he might have lung cancer and how he might die of it as his "Da" (father) did. As he continues to reflect on his health, he laments the departure of Adam, their resident physician: He was counting on Adam's checking him over and telling the captors that Edward is sick and needs to be set free. His thoughts again turn home, being home for Christmas.

The mention of Edward's Da leads Michael to begin telling *his* Christmas memories. His father was absent at Christmas for several years because he, too, had been a prisoner in wartime.

He remembers how he was taught not to cry while his father was away. He says he still does not cry. But he recalls after his father came home, he woke up one night on his father's lap and heard his father weeping as he told his wife about the war.

Michael's father told him of the bravery of the soldiers in ancient Sparta, how they controlled their fear. Although it might seem unmanly, the Spartan soldiers would comb each other's hair before going into battle.

Continuing his reflections, Michael acknowledges that he and his father had very few serious conversations. He thinks back to a time after his father's death when he felt his father's presence. He was reading an Old English poem, "The Wanderer." It was the story of a man all alone in a desolate, frozen landscape who remembers a time when he had friends, when he had dreams. From that poem, one translated line has haunted Michael: "A man who is alone may at times feel mercy, mercy for himself." This line makes Michael remember his father and his father's faith.

This thinking leads Michael to declare his love for England and her literature, and his pride in having taught that literature. This pride helps him keep his sanity.

His memories continue as he laments being away from his mother, his deceased father, and his wife who died in a car wreck. He feels guilt over her death because he had convinced her to buy the car.

Michael ends that line of memory by wishing Edward, "Happy Christmas." Edward returns the wish as Michael admits he never learned to drive.

Edward then tries to bring a happier Christmas thought by telling Michael he wants to give him a present. Michael's wish is simple: He would like a "face flannel" or face cloth for bathing. Edward feigns exasperation, insisting he is prepared to give much more than the "face flannel." He is giving Michael a car. Because Michael doesn't know how to drive, Edward begins to teach him. It turns out, the car can fly, so they sing about "Chitty-Chitty, Bang Bang," the flying car from the movies.

In their Christmas Day flight, they pass over Europe and into England by way of the White Cliffs of Dover. Then Michael lands the magic car on top of the cathedral at Peterboro. He describes the church's architecture to Edward as being from the hand of God.

Next, at Edward's request, they fly on to Ireland so he can visit his Da's grave. He speaks both parts in a dialogue from childhood with Da. In the end, as if he is a boy with his Da, Edward sings, "Tell me a story, tell me a story, and then I'll go to bed." The plea for a story turns into a desperate cry for Da to get him out of this confinement: "Carry me in your arms away from here. If you're in heaven, will you save me?"

Edward is broken. He cries, but Michael urges him to laugh because "they" can hear him. Edward admits his captors have beaten him, have broken his spirit on this Christmas Day.

Frank McGuinness's long day's journey into Christmas may have echoes of Eugene O'Neill's dark family drama, *Long Day's Journey Into Night*. O'Neill's Tyrone family is in a prison of their own making, with walls of drug addiction, alcohol, and unwillingness to face reality. But neither play seems to offer concrete signs of hope.

Even so, Michael and Edward's Christmas observance offers food for thought.

Perhaps, like Edward, we feel imprisoned by negative recollections. We may wonder why we say, "Peace on earth, good will to all people," when we feel no sense of peace. We may ask ourselves, as Edward asks Michael, "What is peace, anyway?" If we ask these questions, we may be left to find our own answers, as we get no audible response from other people or from God.

Still, if we are able to sing the carols and go back in memory, as Edward and Michael do, there is hope. As we reconstruct those early years, we may be able to hear the deeper meaning of those carols and reflect on positive relationships of days gone by.

Viktor Frankl, a Jewish psychiatrist, survived the Nazi

death camps. In his book, *Man's Search for Meaning*, he testifies that his memories of the relationship he shared with his wife were a vital part of his survival tactics. He also worked with his fellow prisoners, helping them to draw on memories of better times to aid them in maintaining their emotional balance.

From the biblical Christmas story, we may learn from Mary, who was confronted with many experiences she did not understand. As a young woman who had never had intimate relations with a man, she had much to contemplate when an angel told her that she would become pregnant with a Holy Child. In time, she was able to offer herself as "the handmaid of the Lord," ready for whatever would come.

Through it all, Mary pondered all these things in her heart (Luke 2:19) and was able to see the hand of God at work in her life.

From the Bible story, we may also learn from the Wise Men. Despite their high motivation and generosity, they created critical problems for many residents in the Jerusalem area, including Joseph and Mary and the Christ Child. When they got off course by inquiring where to find the newborn King of the Jews, they endangered the lives of many little boys in the Jerusalem area. including the Baby Jesus. After Joseph escaped to Egypt with Mary and the Baby, the Wise Men learned their lesson. We are told they took a different route, they went another way. This can be our experience if we seek to follow the God of Christmas. This can be our experience as we discover new paths for our lives.

In the final moments of *Someone Who'll Watch Over Me*, there actually are three signs of hope, though none seemed evident earlier: The most obvious plus comes as the captors release Edward. Although Michael is still in the hands of the terrorists, two other things happen which show all is not lost for him: First, as Edward is about to leave, he takes a comb from his jacket pocket and combs Michael's hair. Then Edward gives the comb to Michael who, in return, combs Edward's hair. This enactment calls to mind the men of Sparta who combed each other's hair in preparation for battle. So battles may still lie ahead for both men, but they are not alone. In keeping with the play's title, Edward declares *he* is watching over Michael.

Finally, as Michael is left alone in their prison room, at first, he shudders at the thought of total isolation. But then, we see a final sign of hope: He begins to quote from the ancient poem, "The Wanderer," which long has been a source of consolation, a reason to live. So, perhaps he will be able to sing, "I'll be home for Christmas, if only in my dreams."

Most of us probably do not face physical imprisonment such as Adam, Edward, and Michael experience in the play. But we may find ourselves feeling lonely or isolated at times. If those times come during the Christmas season, this can be especially troubling because we associate the season with hope, joy, and peace.

For the most part, none of the men in the play was strongly religious, but each of the three drew on his inner resources.

We can draw on the resources of Scripture when we feel isolated. The psalmist said, *When I am afraid, I put my trust in thee. In God, whose word I praise, in God I trust without a fear* (Psalm 56:3-4).

The LORD is my light and my salvation; whom shall I fear? The LORD is the stronghold of my life, of whom shall I be afraid? (Psalm 27:1).

If we learn to trust in God as the psalmists did, we can say, as individuals, in the words of the play's title, there is, "Someone Who'll Watch Over Me."

---

[1] Frank McGuinness, *Someone Who'll Watch Over Me.* London and Boston: Faber and Faber Limited, 1992.

[2] JazzStandards.com, "Someone to Watch Over Me." www.jazzstandards. com/compositions-0/someonetowatchoverme.htm.

[3] John Lariviere, "Someone Who'll Watch Over Me," http://www. talkinbroadway.com/regional/sfla/sfla46.html.

O Holy Night

The first time I can remember singing "O Holy Night" was on a cold – if not holy – night.

As a sixteen-year-old in our little West Texas county seat town of Sweetwater, I was with a group of other young people from our church. We were walking from house to house, singing carols to some of our homebound members.

I have come to love "O Holy Night," but it is not an easy song to sing, especially by untrained, unaccompanied voices in the cold night air. Also, some of the younger voices in our little caroling group were changing and subject to cracking on higher notes -- notes, by the way, which are equally as high as the high notes in the American national anthem, "The Star-Spangled Banner."

The ringleader of our choristers – short, stocky, fourteen-year-old Bobby Reed – was undaunted. Bobby always preferred to try something and fail, rather than not to try at all. So what if the notes went higher than any of the more familiar carols? We were braving the December chill to bring a little joy to some old folks at Christmas, not to give a perfect concert.

Bobby had learned to read music. He played the steel guitar and sang tenor in a voice which he managed to keep under control at his stage of early adolescence. He was also the leader of a pack of boys his age and younger in the church and in our neighborhood--some of them with us that night. So he was game for singing anything on a winter's night, including "O Holy Night." If voices cracked and teeth chattered, so be it (By the way, the song is difficult for most folks, including adults, not just for teenagers out in the cold night air).

Although the song was new to some of our group that night in 1950, it had been around for nearly a hundred years before we tried to sing it. The tune was written in France in 1847 for a new poem by a friend of the composer. Then, the music and French lyrics crossed the Atlantic, where an American, John Dwight, wrote the English words in 1855. There were also anonymous adaptations of the American lyrics. [1]

The song was in The Broadman Hymnal, published by Southern Baptists in 1940. [2] These songbooks were in the pew racks in most of the small rural churches we attended as Daddy went from farm job to farm job before we moved to town. But the song was near the back of the book, rather than nearer the front with "Silent Night" and "It Came Upon the Midnight Clear." So maybe small churches with few trained musicians didn't sing it because it was "out of sight, out of mind."

There probably were several reasons for putting "O Holy Night" toward the back of the book. In the first place, it took up two pages, about twice as long as the carols we sing more readily. Also, it was with other songs which might take a little extra effort to sing, music used more often by the choir than by the congregation. The Broadman was published in an effort to meet the needs of churches of all sizes. The back section even included Handel's "Hallelujah" chorus from Messiah. Most people in the pew, regardless of the size of the congregation, wouldn't attempt to sing that one.

The English words are not an exact translation from Frenchman Placide Cappeau's "Cantique de Noel" (which means simply "Christmas Song"), but they are faithful to the thought of the original lyrics.

The tune and the words provide a majestic portrayal of the birth of Christ: "O holy night,/ the stars are brightly shining,/ it is the night of the dear Savior's birth!" His coming brings "a thrill of hope," and weary souls rejoice as they anticipate "a new and glorious morn." The French words point to midnight, "the solemn hour/When God as man descended among us."

The second stanza in both languages focuses on the Wise Men or Magi. In English, they are "Led by the light of faith serenely beaming." And the song admonishes these men, whom tradition calls kings, "Behold your King; before Him lowly bend!" The French points to "ancient times" when "a brilliant star/Conducted the Magi there from the orient."

The third stanza in both languages stresses freedom Christ brings in ending slavery. The French version says, "The Redeemer has broken all shackles" because "He sees a brother where there was once but a slave." The English says, "Truly He taught us to love one another/His law is love and His Gospel is peace. Chains shall He break for the slave is our brother/And in His Name all oppression shall cease."

Among several revisions to John Dwight's American rendition, the work of one anonymous editor has come to my attention. There were only incidental changes in the first stanza. The second stanza mentioned shepherds rather than Wise Men. But the third stanza is changed dramatically. We could even say drastically. References to breaking the chains and the slave being our brother are replaced by "Long live His truth, and may it last forever/For in His name all discordant noise shall cease."

As I grew up in the rural Southwest in the era of racial segregation, I was not aware "O Holy Night" even had a third stanza. That stanza was not in our Broadman Hymnal. In those years, publications from various denominations in the South were silent regarding segregation and the history of slavery.

I was an adult before I heard the third stanza. I remember being excited and pleased to hear these words. I wondered whether they might have been added during the Civil Rights movement of the 1960s in this country. But I learned that John Dwight wrote this third stanza in 1855, leading up to the Civil War, which began in 1861. This third stanza reflects Dwight's aspiration as an advocate of the abolition of slavery.

Equal standing for all people is implicit in the biblical Christmas stories as the newborn Babe is visited first by grubby shepherds who come to the stable and then by men of wealth from another country who follow the star in their search for the newborn King of the Jews.

We see this inclusiveness borne out as Jesus grows up and launches His ministry. Although His ministry is largely among His fellow Jews, He crosses many man-made barriers: loving and healing physical untouchables such as lepers, social untouchables such as turncoat tax collectors, and racial and religious untouchables such as the Samaritan woman at the well and the Syrophoenician woman whose daughter was ill.

After Jesus ascends to heaven, Simon Peter, the frequently impetuous spokesman for the apostles, learns of God's acceptance of all people. When he preaches to non-Jews in the household of the Roman centurion Cornelius, he sees them receive the blessing of God's Holy Spirit. This leads Peter to declare that God is no respecter of persons:

And Peter opened his mouth and said: *Truly I perceive that God shows no partiality, but in every nation any one who fears him and does what is right is acceptable to him* (Acts 10:34-35).

The theme of breadth of outreach continues with Paul, who had been a persecutor of the church. Later, he becomes a special apostle to non-Jews, who were excluded in the early spread of the Gospel. In his letter to the Galatians, he declares, *There is neither Jew nor Greek, there is neither slave nor free, there is neither male nor female; for you are all one in Christ Jesus* (Galatians 3:28).

All this was foreshadowed on that Holy Night of the birth of the One who would draw all people to Himself through His death. In his third stanza of "O Holy Night," Dwight makes this message explicit. Our group of teenagers had not heard this inclusive message, and we could not have grasped it fully if we had heard it on that cold – if not holy – night in Sweetwater.

---

[1] The history of French and English lyrics was found in "O Holy Night," http://en.wikipedia.org/wiki/O_Holy_Night.

[2] "O Holy Night," *The Broadman Hymnal.* Nashville, Tenn.: Broadman Press, 1940.

Christmas Truce

"WHAT IF THEY GAVE A WAR AND NOBODY CAME?" This slogan was often quoted during the Vietnam War. But that idea became a reality on Christmas Eve and Christmas Day in 1914.

British and German solders came out of their trenches – sometimes no more than thirty to seventy yards apart – into "No Man's Land" and left the war behind them long enough to celebrate Christmas together.

This was a frequent, though not universal, occurrence that year along a stretch of some twenty-seven miles which were manned by British forces in the area around Ypres, Belgium.

The Germans took the initiative on Christmas Eve with a band in the trenches striking up carols, but the Brits were suspicious and reciprocated by dropping small explosives very near the band as their response. Still, the Germans were determined. Small Christmas trees had been shipped from Germany. The soldiers placed the trees, decorated with lighted candles, out of the trenches where the British could see them.

Signs in English appeared, saying, "You no fight, We no fight."

British men then began climbing up in plain sight, and these opposing forces went out into No Man's Land to exchange German sausages for British plum puddings, tobacco for beer.

Germans may have taken the first step toward a truce because they spoke more English than the British spoke German. Many Germans had lived in England before the war but were called up for military service back home when the war began. In England, they worked in various occupations including waiters, cabbies, and barbers. One German barber on the scene spotted one of his former clients among the Brits and gave him a fresh haircut.

On Christmas Day, at points along the fighting front, the two sides shared meals as elaborate as rations permitted. They also played games, especially soccer, which were described by one Brit as mostly "mass 'kick abouts,'" rather than formal matches.

At some locations, the unofficial truce continued into Britain's traditional "Boxing Day," the day after Christmas, when food and clothing are put into boxes and given to the needy. In rare instances, the lull even lasted until New Year's Day.

The truce gave men from both sides opportunity to see their official enemies as men much like themselves. It has often been said, "Wars are planned by old men and fought by young men." Planners on both sides have agenda, some benign, some malignant. The strategists on both sides give the orders; the men -- and now women as well -- at the front carry out the orders, even though some on both sides come to see their designated enemies in a new light.

With large numbers of enlisted men joining the fraternizing, the top brass tended to look the other way at first, rather than try to enforce a "back to war" order. But the leaders used this time to review the war's progress and plan for the next moves. With movement back and forth, even into the opponents' trenches, there was some opportunity to spy on each other.

Time with those who were labeled as enemies made men on both sides generally reluctant to go back to shooting at familiar faces. So officers began rotating these men away from the front as quickly as possible and bringing replacements who had not seen the enemy as friends. Thus, the war could continue.

One possible explanation of the foot soldiers' readiness to look kindly toward the other side is that the war was only four months old and animosity toward the enemy was not as high as it would be later in the war. Also, the early trenches were muddy, ill-equipped, and generally uncomfortable. All this contributed to the reluctance to fight.

There is a post script to this unorthodox war stoppage. At Christmas 1999, eighty-five years after the original soldiers laid down their arms for a season, a British group sought to create and endure physical conditions similar to 1914. Known as The Khaki Chums, nine men went to one of the actual sites of the Christmas Truce and spent nine days and nights. They dug trenches about two and a half feet deep, the approximate dimensions of the 1914 trenches. Sandbags were stacked to provide proper height, and old doors were laid across the sandbags as the roof or covering. True to 1914, it rained and the trenches were muddy. Water had to be baled out almost constantly.

The nine from 1999 slept or tried to sleep by turns. They

also ate military rations, wore period clothing and carried weapons, tools, and other equipment from 1914. At the end of their stay, they filled in the trenches and tried to restore the site, leaving it much as they had found it.

As they completed the clean-up, the Chums used two planks to form a cross, and set it up in the mud in memory of the truce, assuming local residents would remove it when they surveyed what the Chums had left behind. They learned, instead, that local people had treated the boards with wood preservative and set the cross in concrete for later generations to see and learn about the Christmas Truce.

The project drew notice and sympathy from area residents and international news media. Media attention was a stated goal. The Khaki Chums were not doing this as a lark or simply to attract attention. They are an ongoing organization whose official name is The Association for Military Remembrance. With membership by invitation only, the men are authors, collectors and historians who do serious research to benefit ex-service personnel.

Two stated goals of the Chums are to raise money for ex-service charities and to experience some of the life of the soldier "first hand."

These two goals are noble. Men and women who have served their nation in the military deserve compensation when they return to civilian life. They also deserve our understanding regarding what they have endured.

A third goal – more lengthy in its statement – deserves special attention:

"At Christmastime when everyone enjoys themselves and drinks too much and eats too much and everyone has lots of presents, we hope that everyone will stop, just for one minute, and spare a thought for all those who fought here and died here."

As that third goal implies, we know many people consider Christmas a license for gluttony, drunkenness, and spending beyond their means. The sober appeal is for sober consideration of the sacrifices military personnel have made. To that general appeal, we add the Christian appeal to consider our responsibility as stewards of our bodies as well as our budgets during the Christmas season.

Looking back to the Christmas Truce of 1914, we realize there was something which made many soldiers, both German and British, feel they could and should put down their arms, stop their killing. They were under orders to fulfill a task not consistent with celebrating the birth of Jesus.

Christmas celebrates the angels' message of peace on earth, good will to all (Luke 2:14). Christians see Jesus as the fulfillment of Isaiah's vision of the coming one whose name would be called *Wonderful Counsellor, the Mighty God, the Everlasting Father, the Prince of Peace* (Isaiah 9:6).

Whatever our attitudes toward war, history tells us the early church followed its Master in pacifism for approximately the first three centuries. Jesus declared to Pilate that His kingdom is not of this world and, therefore, His followers did not fight (John 18:36). This story changed dramatically when the Roman Emperor Constantine converted to Christianity nearly three centuries later. He then converted the Christian Church into the official church of the Empire.

The vision of Jesus Christ in the book of Revelation is that of a conquering warrior. In the first chapter, He has a sharp

two-edged sword. That sword is seen again in chapter 19. Christ
rides a white horse and wears many crowns, symbolic of His great power. He leads the armies of heaven who are dressed in white linen robes. They also are on white horses. The triumphant Christ slays the forces of evil with the sword. But in both chapters 1 and 19, He does not carry the sword in His hand: It is in His mouth.

Earlier in chapter 19, Christ is called the Word of God. And the sword in His mouth is the all-powerful Word from God. This same figure of God's Word as a sharp, two-edged sword is in Epistle to the Hebrews (4:12). The symbols of Prince of Peace and Triumphant Warrior are not contradictory. The Prince speaks peace, and, by His mighty Word, evil is overcome. Clashing metal swords are unnecessary.

Throughout Revelation, there is conflict between Christ and the forces of evil. But in 11:15-17, we hear the proclamation of victory, even before the final battle has been fought:

> *Then the seventh angel blew his trumpet, and there were loud voices in heaven, saying, "The kingdom of the world has become the kingdom of our Lord and of his Christ, and he shall reign for ever and ever." And the twenty-four elders who sit on their thrones before God fell on their faces and worshiped God, saying, "We give thanks to thee, Lord God Almighty, who art and who wast, that thou hast taken thy great power and begun to reign.*

That eternal reign began with the birth of the Baby in Bethlehem's manger.

Stanley Weintraub's book Silent Night: The Story of the World War I Christmas Truce. Plume Publishing, 2002.

"Khaki Chums," Inside Out.
http://www.bbc.co.uk/insideout/content/articles/2007/10/19/east_khaki_chums_s12_w6_feature.shtml

Taff Gillingham, "Christmas Truce 1914-1999 Volume 2."
http://www.hellfire-corner.demon.co.uk/chums.htm

http://www.firstchurchjp.org/sermons/sermon121904.asp

http://militaryhistory.about.com/od/worldwari/p/xmastruce.htm

He Sees You When You're Sleeping

A LITTLE PRESCHOOL GIRL WAS IN THE BANK as her mother waited in line for a teller. It wouldn't be correct to say the child was in the line with her mother. Rather, she roamed among the bank staff desks arranged around the lobby.

In an effort to keep her daughter in line, the mother said, "Why don't you go over there and get a sucker from the nice lady and then come back to me?" The little girl got her sucker, but she continued walking around the room.

"You need to be a good girl and get back on line," the mother urged. "If you're not a good girl, the bank will take your sucker away from you."

Suckers or other sweets are available in banks as a little something extra to please the customers, not to bribe children into submission. Have you ever seen a bank employee take a sucker away from a naughty child?

It didn't work. The girl continued her expeditions as the mother remained in line.

This empty threat of the child losing her sucker calls to

mind a song which is sung at Christmas: "Santa Claus is Comin' to Town." The song endows the Great Gift Giver with omniscience. Children are warned at the outset to "watch out" and not to pout or cry because Santa is "comin'." Then the kiddies are given details of Santa's great knowledge: He knows whether they are asleep or awake and whether they've been bad or good. He keeps a list and double-checks to see who's been naughty and who's been nice.

Eddie Cantor was an entertainer from the old Vaudeville stage shows as well as in early movies and the golden age of radio. Cantor premiered "Santa Claus is Comin' to Town on his network radio show. J. Fred Coots, a co-author of the song, was a writer for Cantor's show. [1]

That song, which has been around since the 1930s, was followed a decade or so later by "Here Comes Santa Claus." This song was published and promoted in 1947 by another celebrity: Gene Autry, who starred in Western movies and had a radio show. [2] This song also confers virtual omniscience on the Christmas Eve visitor: Santa loves all the little ones the same, whether they are rich or poor. Furthermore, Santa knows they are all God's children, which makes everything OK.

"Here Comes Santa Claus" goes an extra step, offering an outright sermonette regarding the Jolly Old Elf: The tykes are encouraged to jump into their beds and cover their heads, after they hang their stockings and say their prayers, in anticipation of Santa Claus's imminent arrival. They're also admonished to give thanks to the Lord above and are assured that peace on earth will come to all who follow the light.

Both these songs have an element in common with the woman in the bank lobby: They all attempt to manipulate children into obedience with deliberate misinformation. The mother's tactics are a poor approach to discipline for a young child. The songs ascribing divine omniscience to Santa Clause contain faulty theology.

Neither song purports to be religious as such. Both were written for popular commercial appeal rather than for Sunday school instruction. Still, they convey wrong impressions as they impute godlike knowledge to this mythical Bringer of Gifts.

No doubt, many parents use Santa Claus as an innocent game to be played during their children's formative years. But if there is more than one child, parents often try to preserve and protect the innocence of young children when the firstborn connects the dots after discovering brightly wrapped presents in a closet.

Still other parents consider Santa Claus almost as indispensable to the proper observance of Christmas as Jesus. These adults see belief in Santa a veritable theological issue. They hold on to the description written by a newspaper editor in 1897 and reprinted by hundreds of papers every Christmas since that date. [3]

Virginia O'Hanlon, an eight-year-old girl in New York City, had been told by school friends that Santa Claus was not real. So she wrote to the editor of the old New York Sun, asking, "Is there a Santa Claus?" Newsman Francis Pharcellus Church responded with the following open letter to little Virginia:

"Virginia, your little friends are wrong. They have been affected by the skepticism of a skeptical age. They do not believe except [what] they see. They think that nothing can be which is not comprehensible by their little minds. All minds, Virginia, whether they be men's or children's, are little. In this great universe of ours man is a mere insect, an ant, in his intellect, as compared with the boundless world about him, as measured by the intelligence capable of grasping the whole of truth and knowledge. "Yes, Virginia, there is a Santa Claus. He exists as certainly as love and generosity and devotion exist, and you know that they abound and give to your life its highest beauty and joy. Alas! how dreary would be the world if there were no Santa Claus. It would be as dreary as if there were no Virginias. There would be no childlike faith then, no poetry, no romance to make tolerable this existence. We should have no enjoyment, except in sense and sight. The eternal light with which childhood fills the world would be extinguished.

"Not believe in Santa Claus! You might as well not believe in fairies! You might get your papa to hire men to watch in all the chimneys on Christmas Eve to catch Santa Claus, but even if they did not see Santa Claus coming down, what would that prove? Nobody sees Santa Claus, but that is no sign that there is no Santa Claus. The most real things in the world are those that neither children nor men can see. Did you ever see fairies dancing on the lawn? Of course not, but that's no proof that they are not there. Nobody can conceive or imagine all the wonders that are unseen and unseeable in the world.

"You may tear apart the baby's rattle and see what makes the noise inside, but there is a veil covering the unseen world which not the strongest man, nor even the united strength of all the strongest men that ever lived, could tear apart. Only faith, fancy, poetry, love, romance, can push aside that curtain and view and picture the supernal beauty and glory beyond. Is it all real? Ah, Virginia, in all this world there is nothing else real and abiding. "No Santa Claus! Thank God! he lives, and he lives forever. A thousand years from now, Virginia, nay, ten times ten thousand years from now, he will continue to make glad the heart of childhood."

This editorial is a beautiful poem, written to preserve that childhood innocence we noted earlier. But if you remove the reference to fairies dancing on the lawn, the entire essay could be used as defense for belief in God.

Sad to say, some God-fearing, Christ-loving, church-going parents put more effort into protecting the Santa Claus fantasy than they put into helping their children understand the love God showed in sending His Only Begotten Son into the world at Christmas.

It's easier to do Santa Claus for several reasons:

*He's everywhere – on television, on the Internet, in newspapers, on billboards, and in stores, starting practically right after Labor Day, and on through the after-Christmas clearance at the mall.

*He's also with our children in day care and kindergarten, at church, and in the neighborhood. We didn't do much Santa Claus with our boys. But our younger son, Jonathan, brought St. Nick home with him when he saw and heard about him in all those places.

*Because Santa Claus is visible everywhere we look, it's much easier for our kids to visualize and relate to him than to Jesus. After all, Jesus shows up mostly through pictures in their Sunday school rooms and in lesson leaflets they bring home.

*For us as adults, it's also more difficult to deal with the intangible, despite our deep desire to help our children in the formation of their faith.

*Even in this country, which many like to think of as a

Christian nation, the effort to focus on the birth of Jesus is like a minority report. And, in most cases, minority reports get shunted aside, laid on a shelf, and forgotten.

But, with the awareness of visual impact in our technological society, we as parents and grandparents can provide visuals in the home to supplement our effort to help our little loves understand a bit more about Jesus as the real center of Christmas:

+An Advent wreath with candles along with a brief verse or thought at mealtime

+A creché with the biblical figures at a conspicuous location

+CDs and DVDs or older technology with age-appropriate focus on the biblical story

+Age-level books which include pictures that help tell the story of the birth of Jesus, along with the shepherds and angels from Luke 2, the Wise Men from Matthew 2, and Mary and Joseph in chapters 1 and 2 from both Luke and Matthew.

It's worth the effort to keep oncoming generations informed of the good news, old but ever new.

---

[1] "Santa Claus is Comin' to Town by Eddie Cantor," *Songfacts*, www.songfacts.com/detail.php?id=2423

[2] "Here Comes Santa Claus 60th Anniversary," Gene Autry Centennial, 1907-2007. www.autry.com/clubhouse/christmas/geneautry_hcscsong.html

[3] Francis Pharcellus Church, "Yes, Virginia, there is a Santa Claus," www.newseum.org/yesvirginia

Rum-a-Pum-Pum

THE STORY OF THE BIRTH OF JESUS is so full of wonder. It stirs the imagination. At times, that imagination runs wild, as the following examples show:

*As a babe in the cradle, Jesus spoke words understandable to the adults around Him. He defended Mary, who bore Him as a virgin mother, against those who accused her of unchastity.

*When Jesus was seven years old, He fashioned birds from clay. Then He breathed life into the birds, and they flew away.

*Animals speak with human voices each year at midnight on Christmas Eve, acknowledging the newborn Son of God.

*The unspecified number of astrologers who followed the star of Bethlehem were transformed through imagination into Three Kings.

*A fourth king missed connections with the Three Kings but spent his life searching for the King of the Jews. "The Story of the Other Wise Man" was written by Henry Van Dyke (*See his journeys on pages ___ in this book.*).

*The Three Kings came to the stable the same night as the

shepherds at the birth of Jesus.

*A crippled lad named Amahl joins the Kings on their pilgrimage when he is healed by faith after hearing their story of the Child they seek. His story is told in Gian Carlo Minotti's one-act opera, *Amahl and the Night Visitors*.

Another child who shows up at the stable, through the power of our imagination, is a little boy who brings his drum and wants to play for Baby Jesus.

This lad is the central figure in the song, "The Little Drummer Boy." Several different people have been credited as writers of the lyrics and music: Katherine K. Davis, Harry Simone, Jack Halloran, and Henry Onorati. It is said to have been written in its present form in 1941. However, it was not recorded and released to the public until 1958.* In the half-century or so since it was recorded, the song has found its niche among Christmas songs with enduring popularity.

Told in first person by the drummer, each line of the story is enveloped in verbal representations of drumbeats: the highly repetitious "rum-a-pum-pum."

In the first stanza, the boy is invited to join others who are bringing their finest gifts as they go to see the Newborn King. They plan to lay their gifts at His feet as their means of honoring Him.

Self-conscious about having nothing tangible to offer the mother on behalf of her Son, the boy, in the second stanza, asks whether he might play his drum.

The third and final stanza tells the responses from Mary and the Baby as the lad plays his drum:

Mary nods approval. As he plays, the ox and lamb wag their tails, keeping time to the rhythm. The boy plays his drum, offering the Newborn King his best licks. As the sound of the drum reaches the Baby's ears, He seems to look toward the sound and smile at the boy and his drum.

There is a profound thought here which should not be drowned out by the rum-a-pum-pums.

Let us use *our* imagination:

The drummer is at the manger, almost hidden from view by the regal Kings from the East. He is self-conscious as they place their gold, frankincense, and myrrh on the ground before the Baby.

His drum is strapped around his neck, as it always is when he goes about. But he has absolutely nothing to place alongside the costly gifts from the Kings, nothing he can offer the little Baby King.

As the boy thinks it over, he is relieved that he has nothing. Anything he has ever owned in his whole life would look shoddy by comparison. He wonders what led him here in the first place. But here he is, for good or ill. Just then, the woman looks his way. He doesn't know her thoughts amid the strange and wonderful happenings tonight. As the boy looks around, he feels he is no more out of place than those ragged, dirty, smelly shepherds who have gathered around, wide-eyed and open-mouthed, as they look at the Baby and His parents. It's the Kings who make the drummer uneasy. And the Baby they call King.

Earlier, he heard the shepherds talking among themselves – about angels and bright lights on the hillside beyond the little town of Bethlehem, how the angels told them to come to town and hunt this Baby whose coming is good news to everyone, for shepherds and, perhaps, he thought, even for a boy with a drum.

With all the to-do of the Kings, dressed in their elaborate robes as they bring expensive presents, the lad isn't sure what he should do or could do. Maybe he ought to slip away quietly and play his drum to himself as he heads for home.

He loves to play his drum, and he's been told, lots of times, that he's good with it. Oh, sometimes his mother gets on him for playing so loudly while she's cooking and doing housework. When that happens, he drifts out along the dirt road of the village, playing his drum as he goes. That's when he gets lots of compliments. An old man down the street has helped him learn different rhythms. A couple of times, the old man even let him keep time on his drum when some other men were playing their lyres and pipes. That helped him gain confidence.

At the manger, as he's wondering whether he should leave, a thought flashes through his mind: He does have one thing he could offer the Little King. He could play his drum. But then, he thinks; the woman and man might frown and tell him to stop the noise and get out of their way, just like his mother when she wants some peace and quiet. Well, should he offer to play, or not?

Yes.

No.

Yes.

No.

Yes!

The man and woman look up at the shepherds and the Kings and then right at him.

Now's his chance. So he asks, hurriedly: "Shall-I-play-for-you-and-your-little-boy? On-my-drum-I-mean."

The man smiles. The woman nods her head, as if to say, "Go ahead."

So he starts playing, playing with all his might. One or two of the shepherds join him, slapping their knees and bellies as he does some special licks he learned from the old man down the street. He plays and plays, giving it his very best. Everybody in the stable seems to be in rhythm. A passerby stops to look in, then starts snapping his fingers, trying to keep up with the drummer. Feet are tapping. Even one of the Kings is patting his hands together.

For moments, the boy forgets where he is as he pours himself into his rhythms. Then he happens to glance down at the Baby. "He's looking at me! He's looking at me!" the boy thinks. "Can you believe it? He's smiling! The Little King is smiling. He's smiling at me! He likes my drum!"

Then he stops playing. Everyone is silent. Nobody moves or says anything for several seconds.

Then he hears applause. People gather around him, patting him on the back.

"Great rhythm."

"Good show."

"How long you been playin'?" one of the shepherds asks.

The drummer is speechless. He feels almost outside himself as he continues looking at the Little King and His parents. As the others drift into the night, the Drummer still stands, still looking in awe at the family in the stable.

Finally, he puts his sticks in his belt and turns to go. But then, he feels a firm hand on his shoulder. He looks up into the kind, steady eyes of the man. "Thank you, young man. Thank you very much."

"Oh, no," the boy says. "Thank *you*, sir. Thank *you* for letting me play for your little boy."

As the woman begins wrapping the Baby more securely in the wide bands of cloth, she, too, thanks the drummer. "That was so special. Thank you for coming to see us tonight. When he's old enough to understand, we will tell our son what you did."

"I wish I had something I could leave with you."

"Oh, you do. You do. You've given something special. You gave us a memory we will long cherish. The sound of your rhythms will linger in our minds longer than you imagine. You gave him a truly unique gift, something only you could give."

Those words ring in the drummer's ears as he starts for home.

His fingers tap rhythms almost silently on the drumhead as he walks briskly through the chill night air. He smiles to himself as he says over and over, "The Little Baby King smiled at me. He smiled at me. He smiled at me and my drum."

Can we let our imaginations run wild as we think what we can offer that would bring a smile from the Newborn King?

Whether we have the wealth of the Three Kings, the simple possessions of the shepherds, or nothing but the inner resources of the Little Drummer Boy, if we offer our best, we will see the smile of the King.

St. Paul described the spirit of early Christians in Macedonia. As he urged churches to make an offering to some people in need, he had thought the Macedonians were too poor to contribute to this cause. But they surprised him:

For they gave according to their means, as I can testify, and beyond their means, of their own free will, begging us earnestly for the favor of taking part in the relief of the saints -- and this, not as we expected, but first they gave themselves to the Lord and to us by the will of God (2 Corinthians 8:3-5).

The Macedonians gave as they did because *first they gave themselves to the Lord.* This is what the drummer did as he played for the Newborn King.

At Christmas and all through the year, if we give unselfishly of our talents, our time, our love, we will hear Jesus say what He said as an adult to people who gave freely of whatever they had in order to meet human need:

Well done, good and faithful servant (Matthew 25:21).

˙Espie Estrella, "Little Drummer Boy, History of Christmas Carols." *About.com. Music Education.* http://musiced.about.com/od/christmasnewyeararticles/qt/drummerboy.htm

Let's Just Skip Christmas This Year

YOU'VE PROBABLY DRIVEN THROUGH those subdivisions in which all the houses and yards look pretty much the same, down to the identical nameplates on the mailboxes at the street.

Maybe you live in such a neighborhood. If so, you probably can relate to the central figure in John Grisham's *Skipping Christmas.* "Central figure" is a more appropriate designation for Luther Krank than "hero," as we will discover.

This short ironic comedic novel is a departure from Grisham's long-time signature focus on trial lawyers and their clients. Luther and his wife Nora live on Hemlock Street where the conformity shows itself most forcefully in the Christmas season. There's not a lawyer on the block.

Some subdivisions have formally organized associations which require all homeowners to sign legal contracts, agreeing to abide by certain rules and standards.

Luther's neighborhood has no binding written agreement, but the unwritten rules are equally binding, as enforced by pressure from neighbors. Vic Frohmeyer is the enforcer.

Grisham describes Vic as "the unelected ward boss of Hemlock." He exercises his muscle in the public political realm, bringing candidates to his house for a barbecue and circulating petitions for or against various local issues. A call from Vic brings sanitation workers when a neighbor's garbage isn't picked up, and animal control officers show up when a stray dog wanders onto Hemlock. So, naturally, he tells everyone on the street when it's time to put up their Christmas decorations in ways that maintain conformity on Hemlock.

The most obvious sign of "togetherness" is forty-two identical eight-foot-tall Frosty the Snowman figures, complete with corncob pipes and black top hats, tied to the chimneys atop the two-story brick houses.

Other expectations (requirements?) which go with living on Hemlock Street include donations to the Police Benevolent Association for calendars with pictures of local people; carolers from the Lutheran church; freshly cut trees from the Boy Scouts; costly personalized greeting cards from the stationery store; special orders of fruitcake and of ham; gifts to people they don't like and who don't like them; and elaborate neighborhood parties on a rotation from house to house on designated nights leading up to Christmas, including the Krank house on Christmas Eve.

There are also expectations from Luther and Nora's Methodist church and from Wiley & Beck, the accounting firm in which Luther is a partner.

With the annual pressures from all these sources, Luther puts his accountant's brain to work. He does the math and determines that last year he and Nora spent six thousand, one hundred dollars on everything related to the Christmas season.

After stewing over those expenses, Luther decides it is possible to have a good Christmas without spending money on all these things which have little or nothing to do with Christ's birthday. This leads to his decision to just skip Christmas.

As pious and thrifty as that sounds, Luther's plan doesn't include staying put and making generous donations to help the needy. Rather, he decides he and Nora need to go on a cruise, which they can do for about half the total of last year's holiday tab.

It's not easy to convince traditional Nora, but when she reluctantly agrees, Luther loses no time getting to the travel agency and paying for ten wonderful snowless days, starting at noon on December 25.

After they shock a few people on Hemlock Street and a merchant or two who count on their holiday business, word spreads around town almost as quickly as if they had bought commercial time on television. In fact, their local newspaper does an exposé on this supposedly anti-Christmas decision, showing a picture of their roof minus Frosty amid fully decorated houses.

Luther doubly offends his neighbors and business associates, first by the basic fact that he and Nora plan to skip Christmas, then by the blunt manner in which he informs them of the plan.

When Frohmeyer hears about their no-Christmas Christmas, he quickly prints forty-one copies of a message saying the time has come to put up the snowmen. Luther reacts to the message, declaring, not even Frohmeyer will prevent them from completing their plans.

The Kranks' Methodist minister is disturbed when he hears the news. He confronts Nora when he meets her on the street. It's almost as if he considers it heretical to bypass the traditional holiday trappings. Nora assures the pastor that she and Luther still believe in Christmas and celebrate the birth of Christ: They're simply eliminating things which have nothing to do with Christ's coming.

Pressures continue to mount: Assorted caroling groups come to their door, pointedly singing "Frosty the Snowman," to call attention to the absence of the giant figure on the Krank rooftop. Also, dozens of anonymous greeting cards with pictures of Frosty arrive from such faraway places as Fort Worth, Texas, and Green Bay, Wisconsin.

Still, Luther and Nora stand firm in their resolve to go ahead with their cruise . . . until the morning of December 24, when they get a long-distance call from their daughter, Blair, who is with the Peace Corps in Peru. Although she has been away only a few months, Blair has decided to surprise her parents and come home, accompanied by her new-found fiancé, a Peruvian physician. She calls from Miami to tell the time she and fiancé Enrique will arrive at the hometown airport.

The travel plan totally collapses as Luther and Nora frantically start trying to piece together a traditional Christmas for their daughter. They worry about whether to tell Blair anything about the cruise. Their racial attitudes come to the surface as they also worry about what the neighbors will think if Enrique's skin is too dark. They find relief from that issue when they see their prospective son-in-law isn't dark-skinned at all.

But there is little relief in the interim between Blair's phone call and her arrival home. Luther borrows a decorated tree from a family across the street who had conformed to expectations for decorations but are leaving town. As he moves the tree across the street, teed-off neighbors call the police and accuse him of burglary. Meanwhile, Nora goes back to the merchants she had snubbed, to see whether she can get last-minute orders similar to those she refused earlier. She can't.

Luther nearly gets himself killed as he tries, singlehandedly, to get his Frosty on the roof. He is saved by neighbors who are neighborly after he has not been. Vic Frohmeyer, naturally, organizes everyone on Hemlock Street to pitch in with food for Blair's homecoming Christmas Eve party.

When the party kicks into high gear, Luther slips out of the house and goes down Hemlock Street to the home of an elderly couple. He knows they have no special plans for the holidays, so he convinces them to accept the tickets for the cruise. This is the most generous gesture we see on Luther's part. Practically his only generosity.

There are several ironies in Grisham's choice of names in the story:

*Does the central character's last name – *Krank* – reflect his disposition as a *crank?*

*Does his first name – Luther – suggest the 16th century Catholic priest whose recalcitrant spirit offended leaders in the church of his family heritage as he sparked the movement which became the Protestant Reformation?

*Does Hemlock Street suggest an atmosphere similar to the poisonous hemlock plant? And does it suggest Luther poisons his relationships with his neighbors? Remember, Socrates died from drinking hemlock.

Luther's idea of skipping Christmas may have been based in part on concern about the season's losing its true meaning. If so, that concern gets buried as his obsession alienates everyone on the street, including Nora.

Many Americans feel pressure to conform to expectations of others regarding Christmas. This can readily get out of hand, whether in Luther's case of spending six thousand, one hundred dollars, or with people whose annual income is less than the Kranks' holiday spending. We commend him for wanting to free himself from doing things simply because literally everybody else on the street is doing it. We commend him for standing his ground initially when Vic Frohmeyer wants to know why he isn't cooperating. At first, Luther's idea seems admirable, but before long, we see a negative, selfish spirit. Then, when the whole plan explodes in his face, he comes crawling back to conform to the neighbors' expectations after all.

One reviewer [2] was offended by Luther and Nora's worry about possibly inheriting a dark-skinned son-in-law. The critic felt this was inconsistent with Grisham's lawyer books which often show concern for minorities and people in poverty. But I think this puts the characters rather than the author in a bad light. Everyone should be offended at Luther and Nora's racist concern, rather than at John Grisham.

When the neighbors Luther has offended close ranks around him, perhaps we can realize we have been viewing them all the while through Luther's eyes, a trifle unfairly. In this gesture, we need not see the triumph of commercialism. Maybe we can simply see people willing to help a neighbor who desperately needs help.

As we have seen, there is little to commend Luther Krank.

He is, as his name suggests, a crank, a selfish, insensitive, short-sighted crank.

Because of the humorous way Luther is presented, Grisham offers us a mirror to let us reflect on how we handle the many pressures of the season: how we manage our money, how we relate to other people, whether we genuinely find time to focus on Jesus's coming into the world.

Lest we think Grisham is exaggerating the neighborhood pressures to conform at Christmas, consider the case of twenty-four families on Sheffield Road in Columbia, South Carolina, as reported several years ago in that city's *State* newspaper.[3]

For many years, there was strict conformity regarding outdoor trees and lights. Sheffield Road residents were expected to have one -- only one -- live Christmas tree, a cedar tree, planted exactly six feet from the curb and aligned precisely with the similar tree just across the street. Men painstakingly measured to assure symmetry.

There were to be no stars, tinsel, or bows. In short, no decorations of any kind on the outdoor tree.

The tradition traces back to the 1960s when Lyndon Johnson was president, One long-term resident recalled that when she was signing mortgage papers, she noted the statement that Christmas tree lights and an extension cord came with the house---which she later realized was an indication of neighborhood expectations.

On a given day in December, all twenty-four families were expected to put their outdoor lights up and turn them on. Those who failed to conform were not admitted to the neighborhood party. At the gathering, people would tell stories about what their families were up to.

All twenty-four families were expected to turn on their tree lights inside their houses at 5:30 each evening and leave them on when they went to bed.

Families among the original organizers acknowledged difficulty in getting new owners to conform, although they inherit both the lights and the expectation of meeting the standards. With the passing of the years Sheffield Road had no one like Luther Krank's nemesis, Vic Frohmeyer. Still, older residents sought cooperation from all twenty-four families.

So the Luther Kranks and Vic Frohmeyers are not figments of John Grisham's fertile imagination. They live in your town, perhaps on your street.

The ceaseless task for concerned Christians, then, is to look carefully at the way we celebrate Christmas. What pressures do we feel from neighbors, work associates, fellow church members, and other friends? Closer to home, what pressures to conform do we feel from members of our own families? And what about pressures from within our individual selves?

Romans 12:1-2 are good verses for Luther and Nora and all their neighbors on Hemlock Street to consider:

> *I appeal to you therefore, brethren, by the mercies of God, to present your bodies as a living sacrifice, holy and acceptable to God, which is your spiritual worship. Do not be conformed to this world but be transformed by the renewal of your mind, that you may prove what is the will of God, what is good and acceptable and perfect.*

How different would Christmas be on Hemlock Street if the residents took those admonitions to heart!

---

[1] Descriptions of this story are based on John Grisham's *Skipping Christmas*. New York: Doubleday, a division of Random House, 2001.

[2] Nandini Pandya at http://mostlyfiction.com/humor/grisham.htm, December 16, 2003.

[3] Sara Fludd, "Tree tradition losing precision," *The Columbia State*, reprinted in The Anderson Independent-Mail, December 29, 2002.

With Sunny Spells Later

PANSY AND I HAVE DISCOVERED FOOD SERVICE and gift shops are commonly found in British churches. This is true not only in massive cathedrals but in smaller local congregations as well. Thus, a visit to a house of worship can readily provide food for the body as well as for the spirit.

In our travels in the U. K., we've enjoyed refreshment ranging from hot tea and pastry to salad plates and full meals with meat and vegetables in places as varied as the small Baptist church in Bath to cathedrals in Coventry and Southwark (the area across the Thames River from Central London).

The gift shops sell not only postal cards and other simple mementos, but also sacred music CDs, Bibles, prayer books, other inspirational reading materials, and even original art work.

St. Martin-in-the-Fields is a church we have often visited in London. The present building was built in 1726, but worship was conducted on the site at least as far back as A. D. 1222 when it was, indeed, surrounded by fields. But nowadays, St.

Martin's is at Trafalgar Square in the heart of the city and no longer "in the fields."[1] We have been there for worship services and concerts and, not incidentally, the eatery in the basement, known as the Cafe in the Crypt.

On a late afternoon near Christmas, we ducked in through St. Martin's side door and down the steps of the Crypt to escape the winter chill. In the cafeteria, we drank pots of tea and ate salads and soup, along with their incredibly delicious bread and butter pudding.

St. Martin's also has a reputation as a center for classical music dating back to its earliest years in its present building when both Handel and Mozart at different times performed at the church.[2] An orchestra based at the church was founded in the 1950s. Known as the Academy of St. Martin-in-the-Fields, the orchestra has an international reputation for its recordings and live performances.

As we enjoyed our leisurely meal during that holiday season, the sound of an orchestra and chorus rehearsing Christmas selections from Handel's *Messiah* drifted down from the upper region of the building. That oratorio lifts my spirits as few other musical selections can, any time of the year, but most of all at Christmas.

After we ate, we went into the adjoining shop where I discovered a painting by British artist Joylene Lowrance.

People in the painting were braving the rain, some with umbrellas aloft, others with no protection from the elements. I was drawn to the artwork, but I found the title particularly striking: "With Sunny Spells Later." I felt the artist was giving a "reverse spin" to our usual hopes concerning the weather: We like to think clear skies are the norm, with occasional interference from rainy spells. But Ms. Lowrances's name for her painting suggests the opposite.

Pansy and I have never been inclined to purchase original artwork, usually settling for inexpensive prints. And we didn't buy the painting in the Crypt shop. But I couldn't get away from the thought that "Sunny Spells Later" describes the normal emotional and spiritual climate in many lives, perhaps especially in the Christmas season.

Sickness, accidents, relations with difficult people, job loss or transfer, and death in the family are more common than we like to admit. When these or other trying times bring dark clouds our way, perhaps we question God. This just isn't the things that are supposed to be.

Sandra Hayward Albertson's book, *Endings and Beginnings*, tells of the struggle as she and her husband faced his inoperable cancer and her adjustment after his death. She earned a master's degree while her twin sister and brother-in-law provided housing and saw after her two young daughters. As Mrs. Albertson reflected on her husband's illness, her writing suggests the title of that painting:

Likening his condition to a drama, she said healthy periods turned out to be an intermission between the main acts as the disease ran its natural course. She said she attempted to provide longer intervals in the tragic drama which offered little by way of comic relief. [3]

Another writer, Pete Greig in *God on Mute*, tells of his thirty-two-year-old friend Mike whose daughter was born with a serious physical disability and probably will never walk. To complicate life further, Mike has been diagnosed with degenerative arthritis which threatens his career as a hiking, camping, cycling instructor. As Mike reviewed his situation, he said he used to think he had "some kind of divine right to happiness." He said he knew he would face "the occasional rough patch," but, after a while, he found it easier to accept life as difficult and not blame God for the way life goes.[4]

When it seems we are in endless periods of emotional and spiritual rain and storm, such as the foregoing quotes, we may echo the feelings of numerous psalms which are called *laments*. Consider these excerpts from Psalm 39, one of the laments, in which the singer feels the Lord is sending difficulties upon him as he longs for "sunny spells":

> *LORD, let me know my end, and what is the measure of my days; let me know how fleeting my life is! Behold, thou hast made my days a few handbreadths, and my lifetime is as nothing in thy sight. Surely every man stands as a mere breath! Surely man goes about as a shadow! Surely for nought are they in turmoil; man heaps up, and knows not who will gather!*

> *Make me not the scorn of the fool! I am dumb, I do not open my mouth; for it is thou who hast done it. Remove thy stroke from me; I am spent by the blows of thy hand. When thou dost chasten man with rebukes for sin, thou dost consume like a moth what is dear to him; surely every man is a mere breath!*

> *Hear my prayer, O LORD, and give ear to my cry; hold not thy peace at my tears! For I am thy passing guest, a sojourner, like all my fathers. Look away from me, that I may know gladness, before I depart and be no more!* (Psalm 39:4-6; 9-12).

A modern-day echo of the psalm's lament is from Tevye, the dairyman in the musical *Fiddler on the Roof.* In one of his many conversations with the Lord, Tevye points to himself and his fellow Jews as God's Chosen People. He wonders why God can't choose somebody else for a change. [5]

Henry Wadsworth Longfellow's poem, "The Rainy Day," tells us, "Into each life some rain must fall," but we may wonder why cloudbursts come as we long for "sunny spells later." Longfellow also said, "Some days must be dark and dreary." [6]

The Advent season leading up to Christmas comes in the shortest days of the year, with much literal darkness. In those days of lengthening night, as we read the Gospel accounts, Mary and Joseph are confronted by stormy times: Mary is troubled when the angel tells her that she -- an unmarried woman who has never had relations with a man -- is to have a baby. Joseph, likewise, is upset when Mary tells him the news. He finds it difficult to believe she is pregnant by the Holy Spirit and not by a human father. But angel messengers bring "sunny spells" by assuring, first Mary, then Joseph, that all this is the work of God. So they see sunny spells as they travel for the census to Bethlehem, where their Son is born, announced by angels and visited by shepherds.

Christmas itself can bring emotional and spiritual stormy times which make us long for sunny spells later. Perhaps some of the following scenarios describe our stormy spells:

*We spend time and energy making lists and then buying presents, perhaps spending more money than we we can afford for people who couldn't care less for us or our gifts.

*We gain pounds as we eat and drink too much at dinners and parties, then face the New Year with resolutions to lose some of that excess weight. Vows that seldom last till the end of January.

*We gather for festive meals or gift exchanges, apprehensive about whether Uncle Joe and Cousin Cynthia can peaceably remain in the same room for an hour or two.

*We shed tears of joy as dear ones arrive for a few days or maybe only a few hours. Then we shed painful tears of goodbye when the visit ends, wondering when we will be together again.

*We look around at empty seats, once filled by loved ones we cannot see again until the day when there will be no more parting.

*We see other chairs, left empty by younger members of the family serving in wars which have little meaning and no apparent ending. Or those in long-term care. Or those who live hundreds of miles away and are unable to make the trip with only one day off work.

*We sense the return of stormy times after the big meal and gift exchange as relatives and friends are called away by work schedules and resumption of classes.

But when the rush and excitement are all over, perhaps, we are able to look back with gratitude for the sunny spells, short as they were.

Like Joseph and Mary, who see sunny spells after the Baby is born, after the shepherds return to their sheep, we can, with God's help, determine to do the next thing.

For the new parents, that next thing was to take their infant Son to the Temple for purification and dedication. Then, just when Mary and Joseph began to enjoy sunny spells, the Wise Men came seeking the newborn King of the Jews. The men logically, but incorrectly, had gone to the palace. This led King Herod to send out an order to kill all the little boy babies two years old or younger. This, in turn, caused Joseph to flee to Egypt with Mary and the Baby. But through it all, there were "sunny spells later" as God led the Holy Family to safety, away from the king's threats.

As we wait for sunny spells in our lives, we can pray for patience to wait for their arrival and for the faith to believe they will come.

These passages from Isaiah, which Christians see as fulfilled in the coming of Jesus suggest "sunny spells" amid times of storm and darkness:

> *Arise, shine; for your light has come, and the glory of the LORD has risen upon you.*

> *For behold, darkness shall cover the earth, and thick darkness the peoples; but the LORD will arise upon you, and his glory will be seen upon you. And nations shall come to your light, and kings to the brightness of your rising(60:2-3)*

> *The people who walked in darkness have seen a great light; those who dwelt in a land of deep darkness, on them has light shined. Thou hast multiplied the nation, thou hast increased its joy; they rejoice before thee as with joy at the harvest, as men rejoice when they divide the spoil... For to us a child is born, to us a son is given; and the government will be upon his shoulder, and his name will be called "Wonderful Counselor, Mighty God, Everlasting Father, Prince of Peace." Of the increase of his government and of peace there*

will be no end, upon the throne of David, and over his kingdom, to establish it, and to uphold it with justice and with righteousness from this time forth and for evermore. The zeal of the LORD of hosts will do this (9:2-3; 6-7).

---

[1] "The Story of St. Martin-in-the-Fields," St. Martin in the Fields, www.smitf.org/page/aboutus/history.html.

[2] "Evening Concerts," www.stmartin-in-the-fields.org/jserv/concerts/index.jsp.

[3] Sandra Hayward Albertson, *Endings and Beginnings.* New York: Random House, 1980, p. 44.

[4] Pete Greig, *God on Mute.* Ventura, Calif.: Regal Books, 2007, p. 122.

[5] Joseph Stein, Fiddler on the Roof. New York: Pocket Books, 1964.

[6] Henry Wadsworth Longfellow, "The Rainy Day." *Longfellow's Poetical Works.* Henry Frowde, London, Copyright 1893, www.litscape.com/author/Henry_Wadsworth_Longfellow/The_Rainy_Day.html.

Shakespeare Speaks to a TV Family

IT'S NOT UNUSUAL FOR A TELEVISION series to have a Christmas-themed show at the appropriate time, with a tree and decorations and a few carols tossed in to entice the "Christmas spirit."

That was true of one of my favorite series from the 1970s, *Family*, which I rediscovered through the magic of the DVD service, Netflix. This provider brings movies to your door through the postal service or even directly through the Internet.

Family is about the Lawrence family: Kate and Doug and their children; young adults Nancy and Willie; and early teenager Leticia, alias "Buddy."

The Christmas episode on *Family* has some of the holiday songs, beginning with Doug and Willie doing a dad-and-son thing, singing "The Twelve Days of Christmas" as they drive home with a tree atop the family station wagon. Two or three carols celebrating the birth of Jesus are also interwoven as the hour progresses.

But the *Family* installment goes beyond simply a few carols in the Lawrence living room and in a midnight service. The dialogue actually zeroes in on the birth of Christ.

When I used to watch the series in prime time, I always felt *Family* was a cut above most other TV dramas. Then when I recently became re-acquainted with the show through Netflix, those feelings were re-validated. Through various installments, each member of the family deals with issues appropriate for their genders and age levels, from middle-aged adult to juvenile, in believable manner.

In the Christmas show, the Lawrences are visited by Doug's seventy-year-old father, Jim. The father surprises everyone – most especially Doug – as he brings along Constance who obviously is a romantic interest. Doug tells Kate the woman is no older than Kate and himself.

The main subplot involves older daughter Nancy as her ex-husband Jeff shows up on Christmas Eve to claim his right to take their toddler son Timmy on a cruise for the holidays. He reminds Nancy that she had agreed to this.

Worries over Constance take center stage as Doug is not merely surprised at his father but hostile. With good reason, he thinks. Constance has a troubled past, and Doug confronts Jim with this information. The father already knows all this, and he deeply resents Doug for interfering with his marital plans. To Jim, this is a sign of Doug's lack of confidence in his competence. So he storms out of Doug and Kate's house.

After Doug has a private conversation with Constance, he begins to see he has been hasty in judging his father. So, late on Christmas Eve, as the family gathers for each person to open one present, Doug soon excuses himself and goes in search of his dad. Nancy goes to the guesthouse to brood over Timmy's absence, and Willie goes upstairs to his room.

That leaves Kate to console fourteen-year-old Buddy, who tells her mother, Christmas is just for kids, which she no longer considers herself to be. Kate says she felt that way once, but now she knows it isn't true. To justify her point, Kate quotes lines from *Hamlet* which extol the wonder and power of Christmas.

Kate's quote is from the opening scene of Shakespeare's play as two of Hamlet's friends keep watch just before dawn. They have caught sight of the ghost of Hamlet's father, who was murdered by Claudius.

Perhaps the scene dealing with a ghost is especially appropriate in this TV episode, as the ghost of Constance's past marches about in the Lawrence house and the ghost of Nancy's short, unhappy marriage comes back to haunt her.

In *Hamlet*, the king's ghost disappears just as the rooster heralds the dawn. And there Kate's quotation begins:

It faded on the crowing of the cock.
Some say that ever 'gainst that season comes
Wherein our Saviour's birth is celebrated,
The bird of dawning singeth all night long:
And then, they say, no spirit dares stir abroad;
The nights are wholesome; then no planets strike,
No fairy takes, nor witch hath power to charm,
So hallow'd and so gracious is the time. [1]

Hamlet was written in a time when people believed in witches and fairies. They feared the stars and planets were arrayed against them. So these lines say those worries can safely be laid aside at Christmas.

In twenty-first century American English, these lines may be stated more simply in terms that apply to us: There is a wholesomeness and holiness about the season of Christ's birth which drives away the ghosts of the past and the fears which lurk in the present.

Because most stories in the *Family* series are self-contained in a single broadcast, the ghosts in the Lawrence household have to be driven away by Christmas morning. So Doug and Jim are reconciled after Doug admits he was unfair in judging Jim and Constance. Then Jeff, Nancy's ex, shows up with Timmy. Jeff has decided Timmy belonged with Nancy and the larger family at Christmas after all. So the whole family welcomes the one-time son-in-law to share Christmas dinner just as the theme music rises to conclude the episode.

In real time, not all ghosts get exorcised in the space of an hour. Doug's hesitations about Constance may still linger after the presents are all unwrapped and the remains of turkey are turned into giblet gravy. Nancy and Jeff will still battle over who gets little Timmy and when.

Still, Kate's quote from Shakespeare has value. It points to Christ's birth as the source of power to drive away the ghosts and hobgoblins which can haunt our paths at Christmas or any time of the year.

As she interprets the quote to Buddy, Kate says that, long before Shakespeare's time, "so many generations, so many families, so many people have felt that way about Christmas."

And isn't that what the Gospel writers recognize as they tell about the miraculous birth?

Luke's angels declare: *"Behold, I bring you good tidings of great joy, which shall be to all people"* (Luke 2:10 KJV). "All people" can include fathers and sons who need to get back, not simply on speaking terms but on loving terms. "All people" can also include a once-happily-married couple who continue to spar over rights to their toddler.

St. Paul in Galatians 4:4-6 describes the power of the Promised One who arrived in God's time:

> *But when the time had fully come, God sent forth his Son, born of woman, born under the law, to redeem those who were under the law, so that we might receive adoption as sons. And because you are sons, God has sent the Spirit of his Son into our hearts, crying, "Abba! Father!"*

There is a hallowed and hallowing aspect to the Christmas season which causes many who make no profession of belief in the Holy Child to pause for a day or an hour or at least a few minutes to ponder the Christian church's claim of "peace on earth, good will to all." In the words of the carol, "It Came Upon a Midnight Clear," many of us manage to "rest beside the weary road/And hear the angels sing."

After Kate reflects on Hamlet, and the generations before him who recognized a hallowed quality about the season of Christ's birth, she concludes her lesson to Buddy: "Remembering *that* just has to bring us closer together."

Whatever the pressures and antagonisms which can tear at a family, if we can remember the holiness of that night in the manger, that remembrance can indeed "bring us closer together." It's not automatic. It probably won't resolve all the conflicts. But it can be a start.

In another passage in Galatians, Paul looks beyond the

nuclear family and sees in Christ's coming the basis for a much wider reconciliation:

> *[F]or in Christ Jesus you are all sons of God, through faith. For as many of you as were baptized into Christ have put on Christ. There is neither Jew nor Greek, there is neither slave nor free, there is neither male nor female; for you are all one in Christ Jesus (3:26-28).*

The twentieth-century poet Carl Sandburg once told an interviewer the most detestable word in the English language is "exclusive" because "when you're exclusive, you shut out a more or less large range of humanity from your mind and heart--- from your understanding of them." [2]

As we reflect on wars and terrorism and our nation's unprovoked attacks on nations which we label as our enemies, do we dare to drop our exclusive spirit and believe that in Christ there is neither Christian nor Muslim, neither Jew nor Palestinian, neither white nor African-American, neither Hispanic nor Gringo, neither gay nor straight, neither alien nor natural-born? Can we hear Paul say in our day, *"for you are all one in Christ Jesus"*?

We need to be able to affirm with Shakespeare in the season "Wherein our Saviour's birth is celebrated" that "The bird of dawning singeth all night long." Then that bird – the rooster – can wake us up to the testimony that "So hallow'd and so gracious is the time" when Jesus was born.

If we affirm this, we can declare along with Kate Lawrence: "Remembering *that* just has to bring us closer together."

[1] William Shakespeare, *Hamlet*, Act I, Scene 1. http://shakespeare.mit.edu/hamlet/hamlet.1.1.html

[2] Sandburg's statement is quoted by Penelope Niven in *Carl Sandburg, A Biography*. New York: Charles Scribner's Sons, 1991, page 632.

About the author

Lawrence Webb is a Baptist minister and emeritus professor at Anderson University in Anderson, South Carolina. Born near Sweetwater, Texas, he served churches in New York, Florida, Georgia, South Carolina, and Texas. He has been a freelance writer since he was 15 and has written and edited full-time for newspaper and magazines. He has written countless newspaper stories and hundreds of inspirational and study articles in national religious publications. He currently teaches the long-running Baraca Radio Bible Class from Anderson's First Baptist Church on WRIX-FM, 103.1, and online at the church website: www.andersonfbc.org. He and his wife Pansy live in Anderson. They have two sons, two daughters-in-law and two grandchildren.

15599646R00106

Made in the USA
Charleston, SC
11 November 2012